Radek Trnka
Radmila Lorencová

Quantum Anthropology

Man, Cultures, and Groups in a Quantum Perspective

Charles University
Karolinum Press 2016

Reviewed by: Karel Balcar
František Vrhel

This publication was supported by the The Ministry
of Education, Youth and Sports – Institutional Support
for the Long-term Development of Research Organizations –
Charles University, Faculty of Humanities (Charles Univ,
Fac Human 2016).

ISBN 978-80-246-3470-8
ISBN 978-80-246-3526-2 (pdf)

Dedicated to Richard

Contents

ACKNOWLEDGEMENTS
First of all, we thank both reviewers, Karel Balcar and František Vrhel, for the energy and keenness that they have invested to the reading of this book and their inspiring suggestions. We thank our families for their unflagging support during the writing of this book. The development of our ideas would not be possible without the openness of the deans of the Faculty of Humanities (Charles University in Prague) – Marie Pětová, and the Prague College of Psychosocial Studies – Jiří Růžička. Both of them have created a free and inspiring academic environment where the birth of new quantum anthropological thinking was possible.

We thank Peter Tavel for his long lasting support of our scientific work. Many thanks to Oliver Venz and Stanislav Lhota for their kind help during our field research in Kalimantan, Indonesia, to Eduard Petiška for his online support, to Inna Čábelková for checking some of the chapters, and to Jiří Suchomel for introducing us to special mathematical principles. And we also wish to thank all our academic friends and colleagues for the social environment that has motivated us to stay in the academic sphere.

We further give many thanks to Jan Sokol, Zdeněk Pinc, Miloš Havelka, Helena Hudečková, and Luděk Bartoš for their kind support during the initial stage of our scientific career. Many thanks also to Jan Havlíček and all members of the Prague Human Ethological Research Group for inspiring and thought-provoking ideas related to the interference between sociocultural anthropology and human ethology.

Chapter 1
Introduction:
Why Quantum Anthropology?

We are living in a very exciting historical epoch. Quantum thoughts changed the leading paradigm of physics at the beginning of the twentieth century. And, during the next decades, the quantum revolution established a new science of quantum mechanics and contributed to the extension of our knowledge far beyond the classic, Newtonian understanding of the world. From this time on, quantum theory has been subjected to thousands of experimental verifications, and most of its basic principles have been confirmed until now. Perhaps it would not be an exaggeration to say that presently, no physicist has doubts about the quantum nature of our reality.

The quantum revolution has changed the thinking of physics and undermined the validity of classic physical laws. The logic of classic physics is no longer the only one. Behind the definiteness of the local objects of our everyday experience is "something" that behaves according to its own specific rules. And this "something" is an important component of our reality.

Before the birth of quantum theory, most scientific fields were more or less connected with the logic of classic, Newtonian mechanics. Paradigms of natural and even non-natural sciences were grounded in the classic "laws of nature", in the locality and direct causality of the behavior of definite objects. In accord with this paradigm, scientific methods have been developed and used in the research of the reality of our world. But, just as classic physics operated in a specific perspective, the methods of classic materialistic science were only able to explain just the part of reality bounded by this perspective.

Relativistic movements have proven to be an inevitable reaction to this disappointing state of our knowledge. Relativism has expanded in many scientific disciplines, from physics to the humanities and social sciences. Despite of the fact that it brought about more questions and uncertainties than explanations, relativism foreshadows a new emerging scientific paradigm in which things appear differently according to different points of view, perspectives, or observers. It means that things exist, but the observer influences what they look like, and so there cannot be an absolute truth about their qualities.

Not even relativism, however, was able to explain all of the aspects of our reality. Something has still remained unexplained. And, at this time, the quantum revolution introduced a new paradigm and a new meta-ontology into science. Now, we are able to interpret and understand our reality in a different manner. In a manner offering a place for uncertainty, non-locality, and probability. Nowadays, quantum mechanics and quantum theory have gained the leading position in contemporary science, and have even started to influence other scientific disciplines.

Wendt (2015) courageously labeled the impacts of the quantum revolution on other scientific disciplines as even being a "paradigmatic change in the modern scientific worldview". The influence of the quantum revolution on the scientific worldview is evident, but the full impact on the field of sociocultural anthropology is yet to be revealed and adequately discussed. So far, the field of sociocultural anthropology has mostly neglected the important insights provided by research in quantum mechanics. This is not so surprising. One may seriously ask: How could the research of microparticles contribute in any way to anthropology? How are the findings of quantum mechanics related to contemporary anthropological issues? Why is it important to take into account the current findings of quantum research for the future development of anthropology?

Seeking the answers to these questions is one of the main tasks of this book. Man and culture are parts of our reality, and this reality is the same reality that has been proven to have a quantum nature. Of course, this simple statement carries with it many questions that consequently arise. And, the aim of this book is to show that such questions are rather not rhetorical questions, as well as that their possible answering may have serious implications for the future development of anthropological theory. We believe that one should be cautious until anthropology has greater experience with the application of quantum principles.

Until then, we may only postulate some possible implications and cautiously define issues that could be relevant for such interdisciplinary interaction.

At the beginning, the first thing to do is to posit a simple question, i.e. how physics and anthropology could be related? Such a question already addresses the main anthropological concerns. Man, culture, ontologies, human actions, agency, practices, and social life are general areas of interest in various fields of sociocultural anthropology. Without any doubt, anthropology is a science about man, and consequently we may ask if anthropological research could ever be unrelated to the physicality of man's being in the world?

We do not want to state that anthropological concerns should be focused merely on the material and biological aspects of man. We are "made" of matter and energy, and the whole our world is a world of information. And, it is this same world that the findings of both classic and quantum physics can be applied to. Matter, energy, and information are the three basic pillars of quantum theory. In this situation, ignoring new findings in physics would represent the risk of making anthropological concerns flat or even reductionist. The investigation of man without consideration of their basal substances, such as matter, energy, and information seems to be insufficient. The refusal or disregard of new findings from the field of quantum mechanics may even condemn anthropology to lose contact with the perpetually developing flow of scientific discoveries. We argue that anthropology should not shut itself into some inert box without noticing what happens around it. And we believe that something is definitely happening. At the very least, our bodies are physical, and yet these bodies are also closely related with the cultural domain of human existence. We cannot strictly separate the human actions performed by our physical bodies from the agency of cultural elements on the other hand. Just the intra-acting between agency and material bodies (Barad, 2007) has been very stimulating for developing many of the issues that will be discussed in this book. At the moment, however, we remain satisfied with the general notion that "anthropology has really something in common with physics".

If we accept this notion, another issue arises, namely what kind of relationship between anthropology and physics should be adopted for the purpose of building a new quantum anthropology? One of the rather more extreme possibilities is to favor the assumption of the causal closure (or completeness) of physics:

> "The idea is that because physics deals with the elementary constituents of reality, of which macroscopic phenomena are composed, everything in nature is ultimately just physics. This gives physics a foundational role with respect to other sciences … no entities, relationships, or processes posited in their inquiries should be inconsistent with the laws of physics."
> (Wendt, 2015, p. 7–8)

Based on this citation, one may think that we aim to build an anthropology that is meant to be focused only on the investigation of the material world. But this is not the case. When we use the word "physics", we do not mean the classic, Newtonian physics that is applicable to the material domain of man. Quantum mechanics does not only explain phenomena that are observable by our senses as material entities. This may be a little bit surprising for those researchers who still hold an idea that physics is a natural science investigating solely material things and measuring their behaviors. But, in contrast to this idea, quantum mechanics works with the concept of wave functions, and also with the realm of the "nonempirical". This extension of focus makes quantum theory a perspective that is able to describe both empirical as well as nonempirical phenomena, and as such, it could be a science that may serve as a framework for building a new perspective of sociocultural anthropology. A perspective of anthropology that would be in dynamic interaction with the new findings in the field of quantum mechanics. Thus, we believe that quantum mechanics and quantum theory provide us with a suitable explanatory framework that can be utilized for the plausible interpretation of issues currently discussed in sociocultural anthropology.

Furthermore, the position of causal closure of physics would also elicit the impression that sociocultural anthropology should be built on the same basis as natural sciences. However, the causal closure of physics does not have to necessarily mean this. One thing is the scientific discourse of natural sciences with its methods and procedures of how knowledge should be acquired from research, and the other thing is the character of reality in which man and culture exist. We state that we definitely will not follow the methods and procedures of natural sciences here. Sociocultural anthropology does not have a unified set of methodological procedures, but some kind of inherent methodology can be found through the decades of anthropological field research. It has been proven many times that sociocultural anthropology needs its own sensitive approaches for the investigation of sociocultural reality. We accept this long tradition of sociocultural anthropology and continue in this tradition. But, despite this, we believe that sociocultural anthropology also has the potential to be enriched with insights from the fields of quantum theory and quantum philosophy.

The claim of the causal closure of physics gave us the substantial incentive for recognizing the new discipline of quantum anthropology that is proposed in this book. The anthropological investigation of man should take into consideration the physical domain of reality and the physicality of human existence in the world. However, at the same time, the causal closure of physics does not mean the approval of principles of classic physicalism and Newtonian materialism. We strictly dissociate our proposed discipline from physicalism or classic materialism. Sociocultural anthropology has always been engaged particularly with the nonmaterial domain of human existence, and such research concerns could hardly be based on a background of classic, Newtonian physics. For this reason, anthropologists have often adopted positions in opposition to positivism and the natural sciences. But now, the paradigmatic shift in physics towards the quantum understanding of reality opens a new and radically different concept of reality. Moreover, quantum mechanics enables the analysis of anthropological issues that have previously been often criticized from the viewpoint of natural scientists in terms of that they are "impossible to be proved empirically". Paradoxically at present, only a science that has grown from the roots of the natural positivism of classic physics provides us with very sophisticated quantum explanations of non-observable, virtual phenomena. For these reasons, we believe that now is the time for ridding social and cultural anthropologists, as well as other researchers working in other "soft" social sciences or the humanities, of their fear of physics.

Perhaps surprisingly, quantum theory and quantum philosophy have many contact surfaces with contemporary thinking in sociocultural anthropology. Avoiding the situation where one would get the false impression that quantum logic is implanted into anthropology "forcibly" from the outside, we will present here the evidence that a continuity with the past anthropological tradition exists. We will show that quantum anthropology is not constructed artificially, but that this new discipline has naturally arisen in the flow of the long-lasting development of anthropological discourse. This continuity is very important, and we will therefore pay attention to it in the following text.

One can understand the birth of quantum anthropology as a natural outcome of the developments of anthropological discourse in the past century. Efforts to overcome ethnocentrism started at the beginning of twentieth century, which gave way to an increase in the popularity of cultural relativism in anthropology. The relativistic logic of cultural relativism mirrors the changes that occurred several years previously in physics, i.e. after Albert Einstein (1920 [1916]) formulated the first version of the theory of relativity. We do not want to speculate about the relationship between these two fundamental shifts in both anthropology and in physics, but relativism and the emic/etic perspective have arisen in the discipline and fundamentally shaped the further development of sociocultural anthropology for decades.

Another root of quantum anthropology may be seen in the emergence of constructivism in sociocultural anthropology. Very similarly to the key significance of the observer effect in quantum mechanics, social and cultural anthropologists have realized that only the researcher plays a key role in the construction of the social reality that he or she observes. Keeping in mind the position of a researcher, many constructivist, and later also deconstructivist, approaches have started to occupy the field, and we afford to state that these influences are still present in the discourse of sociocultural anthropology.

Also, the postmodern shift in anthropological discourse may be even understood as an extreme application of relativistic logic. The position that "everything is relative" is quite closely related to the idea that "nothing in anthropology can possibly be exactly defined". Taking a closer look at current influential theories in anthropology, many traces of quantum and relativistic logic can be distinguished. The very recent "ontological turn" in sociocultural anthropology is mostly based on the relativism that is pronounced in a perspectival and comparative manner in this field (e.g., Alberti et al., 2011; Paleček and Risjord, 2012; Venkatesen, 2010; Viveiros de Castro, 2004).

Allow us to present several, maybe coincidental, parallels between quantum and anthropological thinking in the following text. Postmodern anthropological theory and standpoint theory (Baudrillard, 1995; Derrida, 1997 [1967]; Foucault, 1970; Lyotard, 1984; Rolin, 2009) have highlighted subjectivity, the individual's perspective, and inter subjective discourses. This emphasis corresponds well with the observer effect in quantum mechanics. Another mark of the postmodern shift in anthropology was the skepticism targeted at science and at its potential to produce objective and universally valid knowledge. This standpoint also represents a mark of relativistic logic, which is applied in a relatively extreme manner during this period of anthropological inquiry.

In a similar vein, postmodern critical theory (Baudrillard, 1995; Foucault, 1970) highlighted the importance of the social construction of reality, and it relativized the stability of meaning over time. Meanings are suggested to be unstable due to the ongoing transformations of social structures. Here, a parallel with relativistic logic is able to be distinguished, as well. The postmodern critical theory further proposes that only local cultural manifestations are available to researchers in a particular time and space. This basal idea is analogical to the moment of observation in quantum theory – the external observer may only observe just the particular manifestation of particles in time and space, i.e. the entities that appear to the observer during their wave function collapses.

Furthermore, the concept of fields found in theory of practice (Bourdieu, 1977) is another example of coincidence between quantum and anthropological thinking. Fields such as religion, arts, or education are suggested to be structured social spaces existing in various cultural settings. But, when we are not satisfied with the understanding of fields merely as fashionable metaphors inspiring anthropological writings, we must seriously inquire after the real character of these fields. Do these fields have a quantum nature? Are these fields informational spectra? Are these fields energies? Can material expressions of culture be considered products of the actualized agency of these fields? Such questions elicit new inquiry and conceptual questions. If quantum field theory currently explains the difference between classic and quantum fields, the fields proposed by theory of practice should somehow be connected with theoretical physics. Otherwise, such anthropological theory would suffer from the disconnection of its theoretical embeddedness from the physical world where man and agency do indeed operate.

Furthermore, the relationship between signs and meanings in Derrida's concept of deconstruction (1997 [1967]) is also an example of, maybe coincidental, emergence of similar thoughts in anthropology and quantum mechanics. This concept supposes that signs exist only in relation to each other. The meaning of one sign exists only in relation to another sign or sings. This contingency is analogical to the effect of quantum entanglement known well in quantum theory. Microparticles do not exist as separate entities, but are always entangled. The quantum state of each particle cannot be described independently of other particles. A similar logic is apparent in the relationality of meanings and signs.

Many other interesting parallels with quantum thinking can be found in ideas of the current "ontological turn" in sociocultural anthropology, also called ontological perspectivism or perspectival anthropology (Viveiros de Castro, 2004). The studies following the "ontological turn" suggested a shift of the internal logic of an anthropologist to some different cultural positionalities (Alberti et al., 2011; Venkatesen, 2010; Viveiros de Castro, 2004). Multiple realities, multiple ontologies, and multiple positions that people are taking are taken into account for the design of anthropological inquiry. This relativistic position is not far from some of the principal ideas of Einstein's theory of relativity (1920 [1916]).

Furthermore, the "ontological turn" also considers some points of probabilistic logic. For example, the self is understood as the nexus of a set of possible relationships (Paleček and Risjord, 2012). This conceptualization implicitly includes the assumption that the self may realize some of its possible connections with certain probabilities. Some connections are more probable and some less.

And finally, the theoretical principles of the "ontological turn" are also closely entangled with the idea of the observer effect in quantum theory. The anthropologist always interacts with the investigated material, i.e. with participants or material entities, and as such, he/she influences, for example, the participants' participation in interviews, and possibly also the participants' experience of alterity (Alberti et al., 2011). Another related example is much more connected to the agency of environment. Paleček and Risjord (2012) pointed out that thinking is partly constituted by interaction with things in the environment. So here we see how the observed (the objects in the environment) influences the observer (the observer's thinking). These examples have showed how the observer effect is included in the multi-layered character of anthropological investigation.

All of the aforementioned brief examples are only some of the instances where some parallels between quantum theory and contemporary anthropological theory can be found. It is not an exhaustive account, but these examples show us the underlying substrate from which the new anthropological theory is sprouting.

Under the circumstances of anthropological discourse at the end of the twentieth century, it is not surprising that a new wave of anthropologists inspired by quantum thinking has started to emerge in the field. In the 1990s, the term quantum anthropology (Pownell, 1996) or quantum ethnography (Vann, 1995) were coined, but no clear delineation of this field has yet occurred. But, after the turn of the century, the discipline of quantum anthropology arose. From this time on, we can recently distinguish several works that may be considered to be quantum anthropological (Barad, 2007; Bergallo, 2002; Kirby, 2011; Russell, 2013; Trnka, 2015a; Wendt, 2006, 2015). Although these works originated from different subfields and were focused on various issues, they had one thing in common: All of these works integrated quantum principles into various interpretations of man and humanity. To be more specific, all of them used the probabilistic logic of quantum theory, and all of them also worked with the distinction between the realm of potentiality and actuality. Also, the observer effect was incorporated in most of these works, especially with a focus on agency, or, better said, on the interconnection between agency and the observer effect. Most of these studies also more or less consistently considered wave-particle duality (complementarity) and wave function collapse for various interpretations of man and humanity.

These publications have indicated the start of a "quantum turn" in sociocultural anthropology, and other related events have also occurred simultaneously. First of all, in 2013, the University of Oxford launched The Oxford Research Centre in the Humanities (TORCH, www.torch.ox.ac.uk/about), and the main mission of this research center has been the collaboration of scholars in the humanities with researchers from across other disciplines. Encouraging intellectual risk-taking and incubating new ideas are proposed to be some of TORCH's core values. Just on the university ground of this research center, Pro-Vice-Chancellor of Oxford University, Ian Walmsley, highlighted the importance of quantum mechanics for the further development of the humanities and social sciences during the conference "Randomness and Order" in February 2015. He posited the key question whether the humanities and the social sciences should further persist on the basis of principles of classic materialism and classic physics? This presentation and panel discussion elicited a very extensive follow-up discussion on the anthropological forum Open Anthropology Cooperative (http://openanth-coop.ning.com/). Many anthropologists have started to join the discussion and suggested very inspiring insights in relation to the new, nascent discipline of quantum anthropology. In 2016, quantum anthropology started to be also taught in the academic sphere. The first series of lessons for Erasmus students, called "Quantum Anthropology and Quantum Cognition", was given by one of the authors of this book, Radek Trnka, at the Prague College of Psychosocial Studies.

All of the aforementioned quantum anthropological publications contributed to the deconstruction of some parts of anthropological theory that were still based on the principles of classic, Newtonian physics. These deconstructions are very important, because they open new views of otherwise traditional anthropological concerns. For example, Wendt (2006, 2015) highlighted the implications of the field of quantum consciousness for anthropological theory, whereas Trnka (2015a) developed a quantum model of the collapses of social, cultural, and political systems. In contrast, Barad (2007) and Kirby (2011) worked more on the discursive practices and boundaries of human concepts, and Bergallo (2002) focused her attention on the quantum interpretation of rituals.

Things that previously seemed to be evident have come to be understood differently in light of the new evidence from research in quantum mechanics. These deconstructions have elicited many new questions and impulses for some alternative views of man, humanity, and social life. These new insights and the currently still emerging issues have also influenced the integral form of quantum anthropology that is introduced in this book.

It is necessary to point out that all of the aforementioned attempts shared a cautiousness and vigilance. Formulations and explanations had the character of indications rather than of final statements, because all of these scholars have kept reflexively in mind that this new anthropological discipline is still at its beginning. Also, for this reason, the content of this book has been discussed extensively with many experts from the field of sociocultural anthropology. One of the serious critical comments we received was the notion that the application of quantum principles in sociocultural anthropology has the character rather of a metaphorical analogy, in other words, that the general patterns found in the research of microparticles cannot be successfully applied to the interpretation of man, culture, and humanity. Indeed, one of authors of this book expressed the same concern in his previous study (Trnka, 2015a). This study focused on collapses of social, cultural, and political systems:

"I will especially focus on the relation of the collapse of the wave function from the perspective of quantum theory with collapses in general, that is, in the sense of a sudden and fundamental transformation of the given system. ... We are confronted with the question of whether we can generalize any patterns of the development of systems on various levels of analysis?"
(Trnka, 2015a, p. 16)

This key question still remains. Is it possible to use some patterns of the behavior of systems on a lower analytical level for the explanation of the behavior of systems on a higher analytical level? In the following text, we will prove that the answer is "yes" due to the legitimacy of isomorphism across different analytical frames.

The idea of isomorphism has already been included in the core of the structural anthropology of Claude Lévi-Strauss (1963). Isomorphic universal structures, called infrastructures, are considered to be a key force for the coordination and regulation of all societies. Structural anthropology sought for invariants that underlie the uniqueness and variability of the observed phenomena. Lévi-Strauss (1963) suggested that common, universal structures can be found behind all cultural patterns, and that universal structures found in one cultural group can be successfully applied for the explanation of cultural patterns of other cultural groups. From this perspective, the idea of isomorphism stays in the center of classic structural anthropology.

The ideas of isomorphism and structural uniformity are not to be found only in the field of sociocultural anthropology, but they are also traditionally accepted by systems theories. One of the main initial ideas of general systems theory has been to investigate the isomorphy of concepts, laws, and models from various fields, and to help in the useful transfers from one field to another (Hester and Adams, 2014). A sufficient level of abstraction is the tool that makes the identification of isomorphic patterns across different levels of analysis possible. Isomorphism is an equivalence of general form. When two systems are isomorphic, the generalized elements and relationships can be placed in one-to-one correspondence with the elements and relationships of the other (Whitchurch and Constantine, 1993). Some general patterns in behavior or structure are suggested to be possibly identified in systems investigated on different analytical levels (Luhmann, 1995). Within the field of organization research, these general, isomorphic patterns are called "system archetypes", "generic structures", or "standard structures" (Mella, 2014). Such patterns are defined as *general and stable models of relations that frequently recur in various situations in any type of organization, public as well as private companies, and in different environments*" (Mella, 2014, p. 35). But, in spite of different terms, the underlying isomorphism is understood in a similar manner.

The possibility of identifying isomorphic patterns in various systems and across different analytical levels means that the use of quantum principles for the explanation of anthropological issues is not only a metaphor. The isomorphism of systems on a general level justifies the reliable application of quantum principles in sociocultural anthropology, although we can agree that such an interdisciplinary transfer of knowledge should be very careful and sensitive.

The effort to identify general, isomorphic forms across fields and analytical levels may elicit the impression that systems approaches do not consider any specificity. And what is more important for cultural relativism in the sociocultural anthropology than highlighting the cultural specificities and uniqueness of cultural ontologies? Paradoxically, this point does not indicate any incongruity between these approaches. The systemic understanding of reality realizes that extracting general, isomorphic patterns does not mean neglecting specificities. Systems analysts traditionally focused their attention to variations, alterity, and variability (Luhmann, 1995; Mella, 2014). Mella (2014, p. VI) straightforwardly pointed out that "*we must not limit our observation to that which appears constant but 'search for what varies'; the variables are what interest the systems thinker*". And, Whitchurch and Constantine (1993) also suggested that the generalization of patterns of behaviors or structures does not cause mechanical reductionism, because these general patterns do not decompose into fractional and isolated parts. The generalization of patterns also does not constitute any threat for cultural relativism and the consideration of alterity in the field of sociocultural anthropology. The only thing is to consider the level of abstraction used for extracting general patterns. Let us describe two extreme positions, a more abstract view and a less abstract view. If we work with a high level of abstraction, only generalized forms are available, and we should keep this fact in mind. In a very high level of abstraction, many cultures may share some general invariant patterns, e.g. ideas, rules, or symbols. When we go down to a less abstract level, cultural specificities arise, and we must conclude that each culture is absolutely unique and that it is not possible to say that they have anything general in common. This "change of optics" allows us to analyze a problem using different strategies, and it also enables different appearances of the problem to be available to the researcher.

Such a pluralistic analytical approach is also in accordance with the complementarity principle (Bohr, 1928). The main idea is that no single perspective or view of a system can provide complete knowledge of the system (Hester and Adams, 2014). An understanding always improves when additional perspectives are added to it. Each additional perspective or view of a system will reveal additional truths about the issue under investigation. As the time of investigation and the number of perspectives increases, our understanding increases dramatically. Thus, the depth of understanding is a function of time and the number of perspectives.

As is apparent, this also has a key importance for anthropological inquiry. It seems that when interpreting anthropological observation solely from one perspective, our understanding of the phenomenon is limited. On the contrary, contrasting and switching between different perspectives provides us with a deeper understanding of the given phenomenon. The appearance of sociocultural reality is always relative and dependent on the time spent investigating and on the number of perspectives used. For this reason, it is suggested that reflexive and relativistic anthropological investigation should be based on contrasting different perspectives and on an attempt for achieving a multi-layered approach to the problem.

We also adopt this logic when we have conceptualized the new quantum anthropology. Quantum anthropology is not closed to the theory and practice that have originated from other disciplines than sociocultural anthropology. The close relationship between anthropology and philosophy has a long tradition, and may be considered to be almost self-evident. But, we have not shut our eyes to the new findings also in sociology, psychology, and quantum consciousness. All of these disciplines share the same concern, i.e. the investigation of man, sociality, and human action in the world. Although using different methods and interpretative perspectives, the object of investigation is the same. Therefore, some of the issues included in this book have been inspired by theory or practice arising from other than anthropological discourse. We believe that this interdisciplinarity will help to reinforce the future communication between neighboring disciplines in the fields of social science and the humanities. Also, for this interdisciplinary overlap, we have considered the quantum anthropology introduced in this book to be an integral form of quantum anthropology.

Now, however, we should move on to the key questions of how do we interpret the new quantum anthropology, and what do we understand quantum anthropology to be? Our answer is that it is a perspective. A perspective that aims to look at man through the glasses of quantum theory. In other words, quantum anthropology tries to explore the basic categories of man's being in the worlds, and for this task, a special quantum meta-ontology has been developed and is introduced in this book. Quantum anthropology is both perspectival and ontological. It is a kind of exploration where the main focus is on man, cultures, social groups, and societies. These phenomena are investigated in the quantum perspective, taking into account the quantum nature of man's reality. This new perspective introduced in this book is a perspective that spreads across the disciplines of social sciences and the humanities. Although the scope of the proposed theoretical perspective transcends several other fields than anthropology, such as psychology, philosophy, sociology, and consciousness studies, the main interest is still anthropological, i.e. the exploration of man, cultures, social groups, and societies within a quantum perspective. Just the basic categories of man's being in the worlds are central points of our inquiry, and, for this reason, we call our analytical framework quantum anthropology.

Quantum anthropology is an interdisciplinary approach, already evident from the title of the discipline itself. Integrating empirical findings and theoretical concepts from quantum mechanics, quantum philosophy, sociocultural anthropology, and quantum consciousness makes quantum anthropology an integral interpretative framework. Many syntheses of knowledge from different disciplines are included in this book, and therefore, we may consider the version of quantum anthropology introduced here to be an integral form of quantum anthropology. Because the discipline is very young, the present version of quantum anthropology is aimed at providing a starting point for future discussions and refinements.

Our book starts with chapters introducing the reader to the basic principles of quantum anthropological thinking. In Chapter 2, we start at the very basis of quantum anthropology, and explore the nature of reality where man lives and acts. We introduce the main difference between the realms of potentiality and actuality, as well as the experience of alterity via a horizontal and vertical shift. The implications of the observer effect for anthropological inquiry are introduced in Chapter 3. Through the concepts of appearance and framing, we provide the reader with insight into the basics of the perception and processing of reality. Furthermore, we continue in seeking the origin of man, cultures, and various forms of social groups in the Chapter 4. We interpret the agency of attractors to be on a deeper agentic level that significantly influences the initial quantum patterning in the phase of emergence. In Chapter 5, a quantum anthropological understanding of sociocultural reality is introduced, and also, some convergences to related issues are signified. We explain the difference between material and behavioral manifestations of cultures in the world. We also indicate the link to collective emotions, as well as to subjective emotional experience, and its importance for the maintenance of a collectively shared social identity. Chapter 6 relativizes the boundaries of the material human body and offers a quantum look on man as a kind of embodiment. Differences from the idea of Bourdieu's cultural embodiment (1977) are explained. Also, the question of subjectivity, freedom, and free will are discussed within the quantum anthropological framework in Chapter 6. In Chapter 7, the phenomena of collective consciousness and collective unconscious are briefly characterized. Furthermore, this chapter also shows the interconnection between collective consciousness and collective behaviors in social aggregates. Chapter 8 explores the variability in the dynamics and processes that occur in the lives of man, cultures and social aggregates. Following Hegelian dialectic, the concept of homogeneous, heterogeneous, and neuterogeneous inner dynamics is introduced and relevant examples are described. In Chapter 9, death and the final collapses of cultures and social groups are discussed in terms of the radical transformation of matter and energy. Here, we continue in our previous work, and build on the idea of the spiral model of collapses in social and cultural systems (Trnka, 2015a). Chapter 10 attempts to explain human language in quantum terms. It is focused on the relationship with Foucauldian discourse analysis (Foucault, 1972), on intra-acting agencies of multiple material-discursive practices (Barad, 2007), and also on deconstructive reading and its relationship to the idea of wave function collapse. In Chapter 11, we show how myth and its underlying symbolic substrate for the maintenance of coherence of social groups are important. Ritual practices are later discussed from the viewpoint of quantum consciousness subsequently in Chapter 12. The idea of a collective body, of synchronization between the minds of individuals, and of the interplay between the realm of potentiality and actuality are introduced in this chapter. In the final chapter, a broader contemplation focusing on the nature of subjectivity and the question of a limited alterity in the empirical world are posited.

All of these issues are starting points from which future developments may arise. Decades of experiments in quantum mechanics have provided us with the evidence for a better understanding of the microstructure of our world. This microstructure is the basic substrate of the same world where man and human action are settled. It would be groundless to separate culture, social life, and man on the one hand, from the microparticles of which various expressions of man in the world are built on the other. We are aware that an exceptional vigilance should be kept when inter-connecting the findings from quantum mechanics with the anthropological investigation of man, culture, and social life. One should be very cautious when conducting such inter-disciplinary synthesis. On the other hand, the new radical shifts in understanding reality in quantum mechanics are so urgent that they should no longer be ignored in the field of sociocultural anthropology.

The traditional anthropological models of man have been rooted using the classic, Newtonian view of reality. In contrast, the quantum anthropology introduced here utilizes and is based on the principles of current quantum theory. Probabilistic logic, wave-particle complementarity, non-locality, quantum coherence, the observer effect, wave function collapse, quantum entanglement, and the principle of superposition are examples of the basic principles guiding the behavior of microparticles in the microworld. We will not introduce the basic principles of quantum mechanics here in detail, as this would simply be a replication of the content of other books specialized on these issues (see the Glossary in this book, or, e.g., Benenti et al., 2004; Saunders et al., 2010).

Very recently, several groundbreaking works (Barad, 2007; Bergallo, 2002; Kirby, 2011; Russell, 2013; Trnka, 2015a; Wendt, 2006, 2015) have indicated that anthropology can no longer ignore contemporary radical quantum shifts in physics, mechanics, biology, psychology, and consciousness research. All of these disciplines have already adopted (to various degrees) the quantum approach, and have started serious discussions about its implications for future research and for the theoretical developments in these fields. Our book is aimed to introduce such thinking to the anthropological discourse. Honestly, we feel very humbled, because it is one of first, preliminary attempts to do so, and we are aware that some issues presented here may elicit more questions than answers. But, "more questions than answers" is also one of the signs of the quantum shift in contemporary science. We believe that a tolerant and open-minded reader will understand well the position in which we now stand at the start. We argue that anthropology should not stay aside the quantum paradigmatic turn in the modern scientific worldview. We believe that anthropology has the aptitude to join in this process... right now!

Chapter 2
Empirical and Nonempirical Reality

The nature of our reality is one of the realms that has been deconstructed by the new insights of quantum mechanics. The former idea that our whole world is made of very small atoms has lost its validity. Therefore, if we would like to think about an anthropology that is no longer burdened by an outdated concept of reality, the first aim should be to ask ourselves how can our reality be understood and investigated?

To start, we can seriously ask what is the role of our sensory experience and its impacts on constructing scientific knowledge? One of the long-held beliefs in science was the assumption that things which can be empirically observed are the only things that should be scientifically investigated. What could be revealed empirically was considered to be "scientific", and everything else was moved to the realm of things that could not be explored using scientific methods. However, this situation has changed. And ironically, it is the new empirical findings in a field of "positivistic" science – physics – that have actually caused the radical turn in distinguishing what can be considered to be "true" science and what cannot be thus considered.

Researchers in sociocultural anthropology are commonly engaged with cultural or social phenomena that are difficult or almost impossible to observe directly. The exact descriptions that are common in the natural sciences are difficult to provide, as we have investigated collective, sociocultural phenomena. It is just this lack of the possibility to directly observe the "behavior" of culture or society that has elicited much methodological criticism from the standpoint of positivistic scientific fields. But now, under the light of the new findings of quantum mechanics, we can state without any doubt that our reality does not consist only of an accumulation of small material particles that are possible to observe empirically. In contrast, quantum logic works with the realm of potentiality. With the realm that "is not here for our senses". And, for this reason, we may try to change our former thinking about the world and admit that there is something that cannot be seen, heard, or touched.

The idea that something is beyond the observable, empirical world has a long tradition in philosophy. Platonic forms, Aristotelian potentia, Hegel's absolute spirit, or Jung's collective unconscious are examples of efforts that moved towards the idea that some kind of nonempirical reality exists beyond material objects. At the beginning of quantum anthropological inquiry, we should try to define the nature of the reality where man exists. For the purpose of building the quantum anthropological view on man, the integral understanding of reality of Lothar Schäfer (2006, 2008) seems to be suitable.

According to Schäfer, the true nature of reality does not rest in the visible order of the world. On the contrary, reality appears to us in two domains: the empirical domain including material entities relating to the realm of actuality, and a hidden, invisible domain of nonempirical, nonmaterial forms that relates to the realm of potentiality. Both domains are not separate areas, but interconnected areas of a one indivisible wholeness.

The nonempirical domain contains the preexisting empirical possibilities or virtual states that can be manifested in the empirical world. It may be considered the background of empirical reality. It is a level behind the phenomena, inaccessible to our sensory organs when they are working in normal, non-altered states of consciousness. Thus, reality has a dual structure – potentiality and actuality (Fischbeck, 2005). Potentiality refers to what "could be" actualized in time and space, and actuality denotes already actualized entities.

Many people believe that only the visible part of reality exists, and refuse to believe in anything that is nonmaterial and nonempirical (Schäfer, 2008). This world understanding is related to the mainstream scientific belief that is still rooted within the framework of classic, Newtonian physics. It is necessary to note that any kind of scientific belief is also a belief system. A scientific belief system is an optics through which many people evaluate if objects or stories are trustworthy or not. However, we should realize that contemporary scientific belief is only another step in the historical chain of attempts to understand the world. Before scientific belief, religious or mythical beliefs dominated the previous historical epochs. And, at this moment, we are not able to imagine what type of belief follow after the epoch of scientific belief will end.

In contrast to the holistic perspective of myths, the perspective of science has become markedly specialized. The body of knowledge about the laws of nature, the human body, or of the mind has expanded so vastly that various scientific fields have made claims on its components. Many scientific methods for observing and confirming have been developed, and many various perspectives of each object exist, leading to the grouping of scientists into subfields within the greater field, each of these subfields arguing with the others as to who is right.

We can picture the development of the world understanding beginning with holism and leading to specialization as a continuously growing image on a monitor screen. First, we can see the whole image – this is the mythical epoch. Then, however, we zoom in on some of its parts, making other sections of the image disappear from the screen. These parts are now outside of our field of vision, they are off-screen. We can still see a sufficient amount of the image to recognize what it depicts. This is the religious epoch.

Finally, we zoom the image in so much that we can only see the individual pixels of color that make up the image. Thanks to our senses, we have finally come to discern the small elements that create it. We have discovered the smallest details, but we have lost the whole picture – and that, metaphorically speaking, is what also characterizes present-day scientific materialism. As mentioned above, the current scientific epoch is changing because of the radical shifts in physics, and also, the quantum anthropology presented here does not wish to share the enclosedness of the box bordered by the range of human senses. The research of microparticles has shown that things may appear in material forms, but they may exist also within the nonmaterial domain. Allow us to show how reality may appear to our senses and internal experience with the help of the following relativistic contemplation about two domains.

Senses shape the human understanding of reality significantly, since they affect the appearance of all of the elements of an empirical reality. For this reason, a belief in just one, empirical reality is fundamentally based on the conviction in the potent reliability of basic human sensory organs, eyes, ears, taste, smell, and touch, because they are the ordinary modes of our everyday experience. Man perceives the elements of reality by and through sensory inputs. Currently, because of modern technological developments, our senses may be technologically-extended. The experienced "here and now" extends beyond the natural field of perception by using modern technological devices like binoculars, or various kinds of microscopes. However, at the same time, we have to be aware that such technological devices are also used by humans, who have only the limited capacities of human senses. So, the results of such technologically-extended observations are also distorted by the primary bias given by the limited possibilities of our sensory organs. Technological devices only extend our limited sensory capacities, and, indeed, scientists who use them operate within the standard limits of human sensory organs, eyes, ears, etc.

On the other hand, there are modes of human experience that have more direct access to the realm of nonempirical reality. By this, we mean altered states of consciousness that are experienced while dreaming during sleep, in lucid dreaming, in trance states, during hypnosis, in meditation, during sensory deprivation, during clinical death, or during intoxication by psychoactive drugs. These states also extend our normal sensory experience, but a relationship with some realms of the nonempirical reality is likely to be expected. Through the altered states of consciousness, we have the opportunity to approach the otherwise nonempirical, transcendent parts of reality. We can see, hear, smell, or touch something that is not accessible to us in normal states of consciousness.

It is reasonable to believe that we live in a reality that has a quantum nature. Contemporary advances in the field of quantum consciousness and quantum neurophysiology (e.g., Atmanspacher, 2004; Mensky, 2010; Rosenblum and Kuttner, 2006; Sahu et al., 2013) have enriched our knowledge about the human perception and experience of reality. So, how, indeed, can we understand the human experience and the perception of the quantum reality in which we live?

First of all, we should accept that we experience the world in our minds. Our experience of reality is extended into three spatial dimensions during normal states of consciousness (Carter, 2014). We perceive all matter and material entities in the three-dimensional space of normal states of consciousness. This realm of experience of the objective space is called "objective consciousness" (Carter, 2014). Through objective consciousness, people experience objective space extended into three real dimensions. In contrast, "subjective consciousness" is the experience of subjective space, which is unextended and contains qualia. Qualia are constituents of the experience of our subjective space. They are products of the cognitive processing of sensory percepts. Qualia may be based on percepts coming from the external environment, but they are always subjective, because they emerge inside an individual.

Carter (2014) introduced an analytical approach including three modes of human perception and experience of quantum spacetime (Figure 1). This approach is based on the assumption that our visible reality is settled within a higher-dimensional space, called hyperspace. Under some conditions, subjective consciousness may be extended to higher, extensive dimensions of nonempirical reality. Carter (2014) suggests the existence of a 3-space, 4-space, and 5-space. This brane cosmology suggests that the universe has more dimensions than we expect based on our everyday experience in normal states of consciousness. Some "extra dimensions" are suggested to exist, but may be hidden to our experience in normal states of consciousness. A 3-space has three real dimensions representing our empirical universe experienced through human senses in normal states of consciousness. The visible universe is suggested to be a very large D-brane extending over three spatial dimensions. A 4-space, having three real plus one imaginary dimension, and a 5-space, having three real plus two imaginary dimensions, are spaces where the human mind may touch some areas of nonempirical reality. These spaces are understood as branes (D-branes) within the framework of string theory (Johnson, 2003).

All material objects are bound to the D-brane in a 3-space, and rest within three-dimensional spatial reality. We see material objects and other people in three-dimensional space. However, the human mind may even experience some elements of nonempirical reality through the extension of objective consciousness into extra dimensions (4-space and 5-space). These extra dimensions

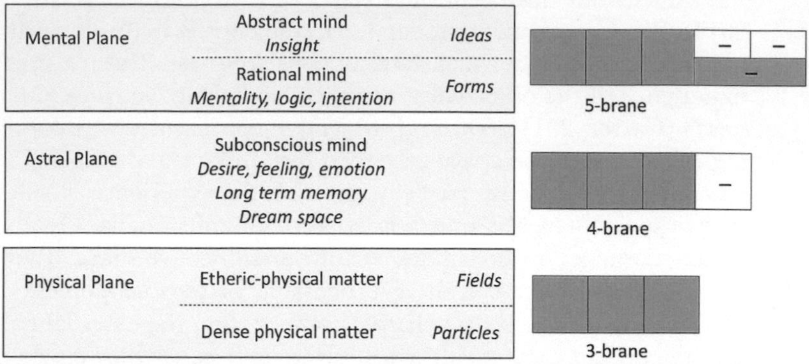

| Mental Plane | Abstract mind
Insight | *Ideas* |
| | Rational mind
Mentality, logic, intention | *Forms* |

5-brane

| Astral Plane | Subconscious mind
Desire, feeling, emotion
Long term memory
Dream space |

4-brane

| Physical Plane | Etheric-physical matter | *Fields* |
| | Dense physical matter | *Particles* |

3-brane

Figure 1. Three modes of the human experience of quantum spacetime (Source: Carter, 2014)

have special qualities, other than those qualities of the common three-dimensional spatial reality. Carter (2014) distinguished two forms of extension of consciousness into nonempirical realities, i.e. extension into 4-brane and 5-brane. As is apparent from Figure 1, 3-space is defined as the physical plane, 4-space as the astral plane and 5-space as the mental plane. A brief outline of these planes will be provided in the following section.

The physical plane consists of dense physical matter and etheric-physical matter. Dense physical matter includes all objects or fields that are accessible to our human sensory organs. In contrast, the etheric-physical realm includes fields that are out of the sensory possibilities of human sensory organs, for example, radio waves, Wi-Fi signals, radioactive fields, etc. These fields, however, can be measured by special technological devices. For this reason, etheric-physical matter is also a part of empirical reality.

The astral plane is related to our subconscious mind. It is the human subjective feeling-space, and within it we can feel emotions, pain, experience dreams, visions, illusions, hallucinations, and have the possibility to have long-term memory.

The mental plane is closely related to human cognition. It covers all of the functions associated with cognitive abilities, for example, thinking, information processing, deduction, or learning. This is the realm where thoughts are generated in the minds of individuals. Carter (2014) distinguishes the abstract mind (in

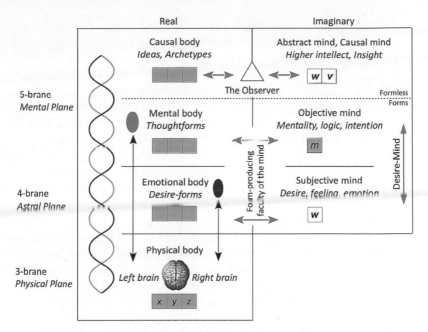

Figure 2. Interaction between mind and consciousness in quantum spacetime (Source: Carter, 2014)

the sense of Platonic ideas) and the rational (objective) mind (in the sense of Platonic forms). The abstract mind is suggested to be a higher (imaginary) realm and is considered to be formless. In contrast, the lower, rational mind contains forms.

Carter (2014) has further developed these ideas into a more comprehensive framework of the interaction between mind and consciousness in quantum spacetime (Figure 2). This framework integrates the previously introduced understandings of reality with other concepts coming from various fields of psychology, anatomy, and cognitive anthropology. The bottom layer of the model, the physical plane, represents the field where classic physics, anatomy, and physical anthropology operate. This field is relatively readily accessible to scientific empirical efforts, because it has the potential to be somehow measured and is embedded within the classic three-dimensional spacetime.

The remaining fields involve phenomena that are often not possible to observe directly via our senses nor via various forms of technological devices. The limited empirical observability of these realms for the external observer is given by the requirement of the extension of human experience into other, empirically unobservable dimensions, such as 4-brane and 5-brane. In other words, the experience of the astral plane and the mental plane requires the extension of human consciousness into dimensions that have the character of higher-dimensional branes within the four- or five-dimensional paradigm (Carter, 2014). The physical plane, the astral plane, and the mental plane are three superimposed (interpenetrating) spaces where man's perception and experience may operate. This model implies that some dimensions of reality are empirically unobservable and represent hidden structures of spacetime.

The concept of extension is very fruitful for the development of the quantum anthropology presented here. The physical, astral, and mental plane are modes of experience of man's being in the world. The human mind may experience some elements of nonempirical reality through the extension of objective consciousness into some extra dimensions (4-space and 5-space). But, if quantum anthropology aims to be in contact with perspectival anthropology and the "ontological turn" (e.g., Alberti et al., 2011; Paleček and Risjord, 2012; Viveiros de Castro, 2004), we should seriously ask how the extension of consciousness can be understood in this perspective?

Ontological perspectivism works with the possibility of shifting between realities (Alberti et al. 2011; Paleček and Risjord, 2012; Viveiros de Castro, 2004). We argue, however, that this experience of alterity is of a different quality than experience during the extension of consciousness into higher-dimensional branes. Ontological perspectivism assumes the existence and participation in alternative realities, but these realities are considered to rather have the characters of different cultural mentalities. The researcher should "take it on" a different culture under investigation (Wagner, 1981) and try to appreciate the internal logic of different cultural positionalities (Alberti et al., 2011). We argue that this shift in perspective is horizontal. The researcher shifts their perspective and tries to understand another culture through other people's worlds. Comparisons between the different spatial or temporal instantiations of given sociocultural forms are made possible by this shift between realities (Viveiros

(36)

de Castro, 2004), and create the possibility of new ontoconceptual understandings (Alberti et al., 2011). However, this horizontal change of analytical frames does not require the extension of consciousness into some "extra dimensions".

In contrast, the extension of consciousness during sleep, trance states, meditation, clinical death, or intoxication by psychoactive drugs is another case. We can imagine that both shamans and participants experience trance states and other altered states of consciousness during the course of rituals. They definitely experience alterity, but such experiences of alterity are different, because they often involve altered states of consciousness, i.e., the extension of consciousness into higher-dimensional branes (Carter, 2014). This experience of alterity is more related to the shift between the realm of the sacred and the realm of the profane than with the horizontal shift between internal logic of two different cultures. For this reason, we consider extensions of consciousness to be vertical.

So the idea of the possibility of shifting between different realities brings together the theory of perspectival anthropology or ontological perspectivism on one hand (Alberti et al., 2011; Paleček and Risjord, 2012; Viveiros de Castro, 2004) with the theory of quantum consciousness on the other (Atmanspacher, 2004; Carter, 2014; Mensky, 2010; Rosenblum and Kuttner, 2006). We preliminarily interpret the perspectival shift between the internal logic of different cultures to be a horizontal change of analytical frames, whereas the extension of consciousness during altered states to be a vertical extension of consciousness. Both types of perspectival change enable the experience of alterity, but this distinction requires a more elaborated theoretical conceptualization that is beyond the main scope of this book. Thus, at this moment, we accept this preliminary differentiation in terms of horizontal versus vertical extension.

Let us return to the realms of empirical and nonempirical reality. Whereas the impossibility of directly observing nonempirical reality often elicits skepticism in strict positivists and materialists, the nonempirical dimensions of reality are the focus of interest for researchers in the field of sociocultural anthropology. Indeed, sociocultural anthropology meets the realm of the unobservable in various ways. Almost all research areas of the anthropology of religion (Segal, 2006) more or less interact with human experi-

(37)

ences that are found within Carter's (2014) astral plane. There are many issues exploring the role of myth, mysticism, ritual practices, and magic in relation to human existence within particular cultural systems. The research of rituals includes the study of mind-body relation as practices that make the extension of human experience into some higher-order dimensions of quantum spacetime possible. Various cultural ontologies also differ in the ways that the human body may be understood and represented. Representations of body are different in various religious traditions, such as Christianity, Judaism, Islam, Sufism, Hinduism, Buddhism, and the contemporary materialist "scientific" belief system (Roberts, 2006). The research of representations of body in various cultural systems, ethnic groups, or subcultures represents a very inspiring field for anthropological research nowadays (see, e.g., Belaunde, 2008; Enfield, 2005; Neiger, 2003).

Another field of study we can mention is related to the distinction between the spiritual and everyday spheres of people's lives. Members of cultural systems engage in practices that are a part of their everyday experience and often serve a practical purpose. Food subsistence, production, hunting, gathering, agricultural activities, or shopping are examples of activities that attract researchers moving on the border of two anthropological fields, i.e. ecological anthropology and economic anthropology. People differentiate between quotidian activities and activities that include some kind of spiritual content. The distinction between the realm of the sacred and the realm of the profane is a classic distinction that also mirrors the distinctions between the physical, astral, and mental planes. Humans are able to well recognize this distinction on a contextual basis, and behave differently within the everyday and sacred contexts (e.g., Alcorta and Sosis, 2005; Hampton, 1999).

A field related very closely to rituals and magic is focused on the investigation of various healing practices. Currently, more and more attention is paid to the psycho-spiritual healing processes within the fields of medical anthropology and ethno-medicine. The research of psycho-spiritual healers and their clients focuses both on traditional ways of healing as well as on new, emerging psycho-spiritual healing practices. The basis of psycho-spiritual healing is often seen as a connection to a transcendent, nonempirical reality, which enables acquiring a new, transformed life attitude (Stoeckigt et al., 2015). The psycho-somatic complex of some people undergoes a radical change during their life trajectories. Such changes are investigated on the level of the clients of healers, as well as on the level of the life transformations of ordinary people into healers. The present-day psycho-spiritual healer identifies themselves with a similar identity to those of traditional shamans, who functioned as mediators between a nonempirical reality and the people of their tribe with the help of religious magical practices (Özkan, 2012). In a similar manner, both of them heal people who seek guidance from the spiritual world by bringing their minds to some sacred places (Sarsambekova et al., 2015), i.e., into higher order dimensions of quantum spacetime in terms of quantum anthropology. The research of psycho-spiritual healing processes is often related with the crisis and the re-establishment of order (Steffen, 2013), which also opens another interpretative framework in relation to the broader general question of chaos and order in society.

Out-of-body and extra-corporeal experiences represent a very actual and developing interdisciplinary field that transcends across the borders of anthropology of religion. The experience of "living beyond the body" is not the only focus here, but also the cultural representations of heaven, hell, and the afterlife represent further foci of this field (Drackle 1999; Paulson et al., 2014). It is apparent that the idea of archetypes as preexisting forms may have serious implications for this realm of anthropological research. In our previous field research (Balcar et al., 2011), the adherents of the EMO youth subculture were investigated. EMO subculture is typical with its morbid symbolism. The symbols of death, dying, self-injury, or self-mutilation are often the essentials of a subcultural identification (Figure 3). EMO subculture also holds high acceptance for suicidal behavior and self-destructive behavior, and suicidal tendencies are frequently found in EMO communities. Interestingly, some of the EMO adherents understand the transition from life to death only as a simple move between two different dimensions of existence. They often did not express any fear of death, and they also sometimes even conducted preparatory activities for the move to another dimension. For example, participant Kevin learned that his parents are adoptive when he was thirteen. Then, in his own words, "his life was changed forever". He described this event as a very trau-

Figure 3. The adherents of EMO youth subculture investigated in our field research, Prague, Czech Republic, 2010 (Photo: Radek Trnka)

matic experience. He then started to respond aggressively to his father and became an adherent of the EMO subculture. Kevin and his girlfriend Lia (also an adherent of the EMO subculture) both reported experimenting with practices of telepathy and astral traveling. Both have already committed self-injury, and Kevin also thinks about committing suicide in the future. For him, astral traveling is considered to be preparation for real death as a move to another mode of existence. On this example, we can see the parallel with the idea of the extension of consciousness into other possible dimension.

Let us leave the areas of anthropology operating with the phenomena rooted in the astral plane, and turn our attention to the human mind, whose research has been traditionally of interest in the field of psychology. Aside from psychology, the investigation of how the human mind operates in the mental plane is the core focus of cognitive anthropology and of the anthropology of mind. These fields are focused, for example, on the research of the development of knowledge acquisition, i.e. how the mind interprets new information and constructs new ways of understanding (Gelman and Legare, 2011). Without any doubt, culture affects our most fundamental mental experience, or in other words, both cognitive and experiential modalities of knowing (Feinberg and Genz, 2012; Luhrmann, 2011; Marchand, 2010). Our minds re-configure the boundaries of our thinking and the ways we make sense of our world (Malafouris, 2015). Apparently, this kind of investigation provides us with better insights into the cultural influences on the process of the construction of reality. Our minds work within various models of knowledge shaped by cultural influences, and, therefore, this area is not only the domain of cognitive psychology, but also of cognitive anthropology and of the anthropology of mind.

As is apparent from this short review, the extension of human consciousness is a central process transcending across the fields and domains of anthropological research. Through extension, human conscious experience may be shifted into another mode of experience. What we perceive and experience in the physical plane is of a different nature than what we perceive and experience during extension into the astral plane. The special characteristics of experiences during sleep, dreaming, trance states, and meditation attract the attention of researchers in some fields, but at the same time, they also elicit some skeptical attitudes in other researchers. Human consciousness extended into 4-brane or 5-brane works within different modes of experience, and its empirical investigation is, therefore, very problematic. On the other hand, we do not think that such investigations should be moved to the area of "non-scientific". The fact that these kinds of extensions are often beyond the technological possibilities of the technological devices commonly used for various measurements should not discriminate this area of investigation. Such a denial could easily lead to the reduction of the phenomena of human existence within a cultural system, which is, however, a core focus of contemporary anthropology. Current empirical results stemming from quantum mechanics indicate that the microstructure of our world consists of energetic vortices rather than of material microparticles (Rigas et al., 2008). In this situation, it is not reasonable to refuse the existence of nonmaterial phenomena. We argue that the realm of nonempirical reality is an essential part of our world, and as such can be approached within the framework of quantum anthropology.

Carter's (2014) model of interaction between mind and consciousness in quantum spacetime provides us with an interesting theoretical background that defines the specific realms of human understanding of both empirical and nonempirical reality. It represents an open and flexible framework in which the proposed integral version of quantum anthropology may operate. Despite many thoughts that could be criticized or questioned, this model is one of the first attempts to understand the complexity of the interaction between mind and consciousness.

Further research is definitely needed to enrich this field in terms of future refinements and insights. Carter's (2014) model is built as a transdisciplinary one, and we believe that it provides a relatively suitable starting point for the further development of quantum anthropological analysis.

Chapter 3
Appearance, Frames, Intra-Acting Agencies, and Observer Effect

The domain of nonempirical reality complicates the scientific investigation of man, since we can not use the ordinary methods commonly applied in the positivistic fields. Despite the narrowed possibilities, we may at least utilize indirect data or the evidence gained from empirical research in the field of quantum mechanics. And, research in quantum mechanics has convinced us that the true nature of our reality can not be understood as things that we can see or hear around us.

Quantum theory has relativized the credibility that we ascribe to our sensory organs. But, what can we do in situations when we are not assured that our senses are able to inform us correctly about our everyday reality? And, therefore, could it also be reasonable to ask how nonempirical reality manifests itself, and if such manifestations can be perceived by our sensory organs? We accept that our reality provides us with some appearances, whereas the domain of nonempirical reality remains hidden behind these appearances. We should realize that it is only our senses that are responsible for the deformation of a basic, quantum state of things that we observe. This notion thus brings us to the quantum concept of observer effect.

The observer effect informs us that the observed, observer, and the apparatus used are influences that are always present at the moment of observation (Barad, 2007; Kirby, 2011; Wendt, 2015). They interact together, and this interaction is understood as three intra-acting agencies that are always present when we try to investigate anything (Barad, 2007; Kirby, 2011; Wendt, 2015). The observer effect is one of the main issues that has the potential to contribute to current anthropological theory. It is for this reason that we will also pay special attention to the implications of this concept for sociocultural anthropology throughout this chapter.

We continue in the line of reasoning that was started in the studies of Barad (2007), Kirby (2011), and Wendt (2015). If the observed, observer, and the apparatus always intra-act, then scientific knowledge is thus deformed by this intra-acting. The question is, what is then available to the senses and cognition of the observer? We argue that it is just an appearance. The appearance that emerges in the intra-acting of the observed, observer, and the apparatus used. As anthropologists also observe sociocultural reality, we argue that they are dependent on the appearances of this reality, and their inquiry is then appearance-based. Anthropologists have some appearances available and these appearances are also fundamental for their follow-up interpretations. Thus, the only thing we can say about sociocultural reality is "how anthropologists interpret" appearances of it, and not what sociocultural reality really is. Apparently, the possible objectivity of scientific knowledge is, therefore, disqualified by the influence of the observer effect itself.

For these reasons, we will work with the concept of appearance throughout this book. We believe that the concept of appearance is one of basic ideas for anthropology inspired by quantum theory. Anthropological knowledge is always supposed to be subjective, because the observer deforms the appearance of the observed by the moment of observation itself. It is, indeed, the main impact of the observer effect for any anthropological inquiry.

Because of the key importance of this issue, let us explore the concept of appearance in more detail. In philosophy, the idea of appearance has been broadly discussed, for example, in the field of continental phenomenology. Indeed, phenomenology itself is even understood explicitly as a "science of appearance". The world comes to appearance "in" and "through" humans and, therefore, phenomenology always begins with the appearance of the observed to human consciousness. Brentano (1995 [1911]) understood the existence of extra-mental or extra-perceptual objects in terms of their sensory impressions in the observer. Physical phenomena do not have any existence other than intentional existence, they appear only "in" and "through" the mental act of the observer. The existence of objects is limited to the instance of their occurrence in perception. Thus, objects are given only by our sensory experience.

The awareness of subjective influences of the observer is apparent also in the works of Husserl (1964, 1983). According to Husserl, the observed entity contains nothing in itself but only what appears and as it appears in the "mode of givenness". There are many modes of givenness, and each perception as well as observer has different background intuitions of the entities. The essence of the phenomenon is manifested as the structure of its essential possibilities. The actual world, where phenomena are manifested, refers to the realm of factuality, or, "actuality" in terms of the quantum anthropology presented here.

Heidegger (1962, 1996) denoted the manifestation of phenomena in the world through the acts of consciousness as the self-manifestation, revelation, disclosure, or as "showing itself". We observe the appearances of things, not their real being. Things may show themselves in many ways, and it depends on the modes of access that we have to them. Within the framework of quantum anthropology, the modes of access may be related to our senses, to our perceptual abilities, or to the technological devices that we use for observing phenomena.

Moran (2000) summarized the main idea of phenomenology as follows:

"Phenomenology must carefully describe things as they appear to consciousness. In other words, the way problems, things, and events are approached must involve taking their manner of appearance to consciousness into consideration."
(Moran, 2000, p. 6)

Aside from this, there are also some indicators of awareness of the entanglement between the observed, the observer, and the apparatus in phenomenological philosophy. For example, Brentano (1995 [1911]) pointed out that object refers both to the appearing physical phenomenon and the act itself. Furthermore, Sartre (1995) also pointed out the relativity of the observed phenomenon in relation to a subject observing it. According to him, there are infinitely many possible ways of observing and interpreting phenomena. Ingarden (1975) almost anticipated some implications of the observer effect developed in quantum mechanics:

"We are only concerned to state that there is a 'correlativity' and a mutual dependence between two parallel processes: in the experiencing subject and in the object which reveals itself to the observer and at the same time comes into being through this manifestation. These processes cannot be separated and neither can be studied in complete isolation from the other."
(Ingarden, 1975, p. 263)

Phenomenological philosophy is inspiring for the framework of quantum anthropology, although the quantum anthropology presented here will not use the phenomenological method *per se*. We will continue in the development of these ideas in a manner that is more fitting for the case of the quantum anthropological perspective.

When thinking about man's perception and appearance, we should start at the level of the cognitive processing of percepts from the external environment. The human mind processes reality in the flow of images that consists of all possible sensory modalities in the normal states of consciousness, i.e. based on visual, auditory, taste, tactile, and olfactory percepts. When we try to grasp the suggested flow of images analytically, one can imagine a sort of framing of reality. Our idea is that sociocultural reality reveals itself to the sensory experiences of the observer as chained frames. Frames are suggested to be the basic constitutive moments of man's experience. We understand frames as cognitively created images of the observed that are available in our consciousness. And, this is not only the case of visual perception, but of all of the possible modalities in which sociocultural reality is possibly perceived.

During any investigation, frames emerge to the analytical apparatus during the stream of consciousness of an investigator, i.e. an anthropologist. Frames are chained, so we might expect the continuity of anthropological experience, as one frame influences the appearance of subsequent frames. So, these fragments create a basis upon which an anthropologist forms his/her understanding of sociocultural reality. The moment of appearance is "what is available" to our sensual experience in a particular time and space. And, each moment of appearance, i.e. a frame, is the moment of the intra-acting of the agencies of the observer, observed, and the apparatus used.

Frames are products of an individual's cognition as their chains emerge in consciousness. They are not, however, the equivalent of what Malin (2012) called elementary quantum events. Elementary quantum events are supposed to be atemporal and discrete without any continuity. Every elementary quantum event is new, and its appearance is given by the collapse of a quantum state. Malin (2012) pointed out that continuous endurance of things is only apparent. We agree with him that the continuity in man, cultures, and social groups is constructed in our minds. But we also argue that the impression of continuous endurance of some entities in time is enabled by the quantum coherence of a pattern that appears to our senses during a series of collapses of quantum states. In other words, a series of collapses of quantum states may provide human observers with a coherent pattern, and this pattern is then perceived by our senses, creating the background for the follow-up emergence of continuity in our minds.

Anthropology is a science about man, and we accept man's position in the world as it is, including man's cognitive limitations, i.e. the cognitively constructed impressions of continuity or the identity of the observed. We accept these limitations within our quantum anthropological perspective, and we realize that frames emerging in an individual's cognition do not mirror atemporal, discrete elementary quantum events. Frames are always mere impressions, as human cognitive abilities are not sufficient enough to capture and process the discrete elementary quantum events as described by Malin (2012). For this reason, we accept the way man is able to perceive and understand reality as a starting point of quantum anthropological inquiry. Despite of the fact that human cognitive abilities are not "sharp" enough to possibly capture elementary quantum events, it cannot prevent us from investigating man as a quantum system.

Thus, we have to accept that the framing of reality always includes the limitations of man's perception and cognition. Furthermore, we argue here that framing is always selective. What must be considered is that each frame 1) is focused on a specific segment of reality, 2) has its own, specific range, i.e. a range in terms of the size of a percept – from a microshot to a macroview, 3) has its own sharpness, i.e. some parts of a frame may be sharp whereas some parts may be blurred. These characteristics highlight various features of the selectivity of framing. The three agencies of the observer, observed, and the apparatus are always intra-acting at the moment of appearance, i.e., when a frame emerges in the consciousness of the observer. Therefore, selectivity operates on all three levels, i.e. in the observer, in the observed object, and in the apparatus. The observer selects both consciously and unconsciously what will be observed, and this selection is influenced by the observer's cultural determination, unconscious processes, volitional efforts, etc. Furthermore, each apparatus enables just one particular form of observation. Finally, sociocultural reality itself does not provide us with full access to all of its parts at the moment of observation. Some parts are possible to observe, and some parts may be hidden to the apparatus of the observer.

The concepts of appearance and framing enable us to view anthropological investigation in a slightly different manner. Yet they lead us to the more general question of where are such appearances rooted? Or, where do appearances of both the material and nonmaterial world originate? Indeed, these questions are questions on the possible sources of appearances. One of the possibilities is the exciting hypothesis that all of the variants of the realm of potentiality are found in empty states (Schäfer, 2008; Puthoff, 2002). Such virtual empty states are suggested to have the potential to express their logical order in the empirical world as some kind of embodiment, event, human action, or behavior. Virtual empty states are suggested to be a source for the realm of potentiality. Such ways of thinking may imply that the realm of virtual states contains all of the future empirical possibilities.

All of these exciting ideas elicit many insistent questions. As we will see later, many of them oscillate around the issue of a starting point and are concerned with the moment of the genesis and emergence of appearances, entities, fields, and processes in the world. Therefore, a broader quantum anthropological exploration of this issue is provided in the following chapter. So, let us turn our attention to the moment of beginning, i.e. to the origin of man, cultures, and societies.

Chapter 4
Emergence of Man and Culture

When starting to think about "something that is only beginning to exist", we should consider the instance of a hypothetical state where an entity in question is not yet in a state of being. We may imagine something as in a state of "pre-being", "pre-existence", or in a "pre-existing state". When an entity does not yet exist, it means that its existence is not yet here. Indeed, we can understand this state to be a zero state. Zero state is a very important mathematical formalism, because it indicates an absence. An entity does not exist yet. There is an empty space instead. Zero state and empty space are instances of primary undifferentiatedness. These instances constitute the initial conditions before an existence starts. Therefore, we should take them into account before proceeding further to the idea that something is emerging.

Quantum systems behave in accordance with the Parmenidian principle, which posits that a system needs empty states in order to be able to change (Schäfer, 2006). In contrast, the imagery situation, when all of the states of all of the systems in the universe would be occupied and completely filled, would cause the end of perpetual changes in all of systems in time and space. Therefore, when searching for a primary source for possible actualizations of quantum potentiality, one may think of the idea of an all-pervasive set of quantum possibilities. One of the concepts attempting to hypothesize such a set is Puthoff's quantum sea of zero-point fluctuations (2002).

In physics, Puthoff's quantum sea (2002) is a single underlying substructure that is common for the entire universe, and represents a source for all actualizations in time and space. It is a quantum field of potentiality. This underlying substructure consists of so-called zero-point fluctuations of fields, like the electromagnetic field. The all-pervasive energetic field called quantum vacuum energy, or zero-point energy, is a random, ambient fluctuating energy that exists even in so-called empty space. The sustainment of zero-point energy is continually being absorbed and re-emitted on a dynamic-balance basis.

Microparticles have certain qualities when observed under real-life conditions. The observer can determine such qualities of a microparticle as specific spin, the frequency of oscillation/amplitude, its angular momentum, magnetic moment, and electrical charge at the moment of measurement. Simply said, each microparticle is a very small energetic vortex that has its own qualities. Another situation arises when thinking about zero-point fluctuations in a vacuum. A vacuum is never particle- or field-free, but consists of continuous virtual particle-pair creation and annihilation. There are fleeting electromagnetic waves and pairs of microparticles that perpetually come into being and return back again into nonexistence. Energy patterns like material entities or other entities emerge as a result of the patterning of otherwise random, ambient zero-point energy. We understand this dynamic substrate as an overall energy-information potential for any actualization (Trnka, 2015a). When an entity is emerging, it means that a part of the quantum sea has started to be manifested (actualized) in time and space.

In our previous anthropological study (Trnka, 2015a), the term "overall, wave-particle energy-information potential" was introduced. The basic idea of the overall energy-information potential is very similar to the idea of Puthoff's quantum sea (2002) emerging in physics. It was also suggested that overall, wave-particle energy-information potential is an underlying all-pervasive substructure that provides energy-information potential for all actualizations in time and space. Such actualizations may be material or nonmaterial entities, and some of them may be observed by human observers whereas others are not. The concept of the overall energy-information potential also accepts that the qualities of microparticles in a vacuum serve as pre-existing information for future actualizations. It other words, zero-point fluctuations in the vacuum serve as a primary source for all actualizations in time and space, both material and nonmaterial.

When considering material entities, human bodies as well as any other material objects are actualizations of some parts of the overall energy-information potential. Therefore, they share a common source – in other words, they are born from zero-point fluctuations in the vacuum. Such ambient zero-point energies are suggested to be random and maybe, because of this, human bodies are so unique that it is almost impossible to find two people who are absolutely the same in terms of their psyche, anatomy, physiology, or the functioning of their nervous systems. Analogically, it is impossible to find two absolutely same cultures or societies. This variability is primarily given by the complexity of these systems. Both internal (inside the system) and external (system versus its environment) differentiation proceeds perpetually in all highly complex systems (Luhmann, 1995). But, aside of changing throughout the life of complex systems, high variability is also related to the initial conditions at the moment of emergence. And, when taking into account the character of overall energy-information potential, we should also ask about the nature of the initial patterning of entities from zero-point fluctuations in the vacuum.

We argue that there is something, which could be considered to be responsible for the initial variability during the emergence of various entities. The term attractor is widely used within the field of mathematical modeling, which describes the constellation towards which a system tends to move. In psychology, an attractor is generally defined as an equilibrium state or cycle of states into which a system settles over time (Arrow and Burns, 2004). This understanding implies that the hypothetical assumption of a state that attracts the behavior of a system is responsible for a system's development and differentiation in time and space. Here, however, we also extend the role of attractors to the moment of emergence. Before any entity starts to exist, zero-point fluctuations in the vacuum are suggested to be random and chaotic. When some entity is coming into being, we argue that some kind of quantum patterning begins to operate. And, such quantum patterning is not supposed to be random, but it is hypothesized to be attracted by some kind of attractor. Thus, an attractor is initial information for new, arising form.

But here, we may ask ourselves what implications does the consideration of attractors have for sociocultural anthropological theory? The issue of agency has been frequently discussed in the field of sociocultural anthropology (e.g. Bourdieu, 1977; Holland et al., 2003; Kockelman, 2007) and agency has been found to be mostly associated with some kind of human action or the action of human products in the world. In contrast, less attention has been paid to the emergence of man, cultures, and social aggregates. However, a better understanding of cultures and social aggregates also requires a better understanding of the initial conditions at the moment of emergence. We argue here that all emergence is related to the operation of various kinds of attractor. And therefore, we also posit the suggestion, that man, cultures, and various forms of social life are attracted by the agency of attractors at the moment of their emergence. We redefine attractors to be agentic constellations that are responsible for the initial variability among individuals as well as among forms of social coherence. When an entity comes into existence from the overall energy-information potential, the agency of some kind of attractor starts to act. It is "agency beyond agency", because it acts without the agency of human action or the action of human products in the world. A deeper agentic level that operates out of human activity is suggested to exist. But, this deep, underlying agency must be present, because otherwise, the appearance of all entities would be as random as primary zero-point fluctuations are. And it is obvious that people, animals, and plants are not absolutely random. Despite the initial variability of quantum sea, the appearances of these are coherent enough that we, external observers, can identify man as man (not as a plant), and animals as animals. For these reasons, we introduce the concept of attractor to sociocultural anthropology here and we will later show in this chapter various instances proving why the consideration of attractors is essential when exploring the emergence of man, cultures, and social aggregates. We argue that the emergence of entities and systems from the quantum sea of possibilities is influenced by attractors that are responsible for concrete actualizations in time and space.

Let us begin at the simplest level of anthropological inquiry, at the stage of the biological conception of a new person. We are aware that this issue falls mostly under the field of biological anthropology and not sociocultural anthropology, but we do not want to omit it only because of its disciplinary situating. Before the conception of a new human embryo, there are two haploid cells at the beginning, an ovum and a sperm. Both sperms and human ova emerge in the process of oogenesis (to be specific, spermatogenesis in males and primordial folliculogenesis in females). It is this very moment when new human reproductive cells emerge as actualizations of some parts of the overall energy-information potential.

We may expect that the genesis of primordial germ cells share similar rules to nonlinear quantum systems in general. Isaeva (2012) suggested that the dynamics of biological systems as nonlinear quantum systems is linked with some kinds of strange attractors. These strange attractors have a fractal structure, typically include chaotic dynamics, and have sensitive dependence on initial conditions. The self-organization processes of cytoskeleton system play a key role in primordial oogenesis. The cytoskeleton itself is suggested to be a generator of further morphogenesis:

"During ooplasmic egg segregation, which is a key process for establishing axis polarity of a new organism, the cytoskeleton of an egg cell functions as the global morphogenetic determinant, which directs and fixes the anisotropy of molecular information distribution in the ooplasm."
(Isaeva, 2012, p. 113)

When searching for strange attractors that are responsible for primordial oogenesis, we can explore the initial conditions that influence the emergence and follow up the development of primordial germ cells. This means topological attractors, physical attractors, and possibly also gene regulatory networks' attractors (Isaeva, 2012). The topological attractors involve the heterogeneous distribution of structural components, ion flows and electric fields, fields of mechanical tensions, transcellular transport, or intercellular movements, and signaling. These topological attractors have the character of scalar or vector fields. Furthermore, physical attractors are also physical restrictions, for example, gravitation vectors, physical gradients of the environment, or mechanical stress. It is also possible that extracellular gene regulatory networks may influence the genesis of new germ cells in oogenesis, at least to some extent.

This small excursion into biological anthropology showed us that even with this relatively simple case of emergence, many influences play a role when trying to understand the constellation of the initial conditions for the emergence of a new person. We can imagine that the aforementioned influences combined together may create myriads of variants of initial conditions in time and space. Taken together, all of the above-mentioned attractors may be linked with the emergence of new sperm, of ovarian follicles, but also of primordial cellular consciousness. The question arises whether just one strange attractor consisting of these influences is responsible for the emergence of a new human reproductive cell, or if more strange attractors may mutually interfere? We leave this question aside for now. Yet we see on this simple example how the emergence of a new entity is attracted from the overall energy-information potential.

The moment of emergence is merely the moment when a part of the overall energy-information potential starts to be actualized in the form of a new, arising entity. Both the new sperm and ovarian follicle are the actualizations of pre-existing pre-manifestations of energy from the overall energy-information potential. From this moment, these primordial germ cells exist in their external environments, which immediately starts to influence them in many ways. But, aside from the influences of the external environment, the internal environment of the cell also starts to influence development of the cell. For these reasons, we speak about both the internal and external differentiation that always proceeds in all kinds of systems (Luhmann, 1995).

Now we shift our attention to more complex examples, to the emergence of various forms of social life. Generally, social systems have the character of multilevel complex systems that are guided by some kind of strange attractors (Arrow and Burns, 2004). The emergence of new social systems is rooted in the thoughts and actions of individuals, as well as based on the external forces like material environment or cultural influences. The birth of a new social system is linked with the emergence of order from nonlinear relationships among multiple interacting units (Casti, 1994), where multiple interacting units are individual thoughts, consciousness, and actions. It is the process of the complexification of individual thoughts and consciousness.

During the emergence of a social system, bottom-up processes prevail in the dynamics of the emerging social aggregate, but also top-down processes start to influence the social system immediately after its birth. Here, the bidirectional relationship between the social system and its members is constituted. This relationship has the character of autopoietical reproduction in

Luhmann's sense (1995). Autopoiesis is the function of self-reference. Systems have their own bidirectional function that enables feedback between their internal and external environment. Only because of autopoiesis is the self-organization of the system possible.

At the beginning of a new social form, individual thoughts, ideas, actions, and initial beliefs start to interact with each other. The fluctuations of thoughts and communication flows have a character similar to the perpetual interactions between microparticles. It is the perpetual vibrating of elements that is permanently creating emergent qualities on a higher level of analysis, e.g. shared cultural standards or norms in the case of social systems. These initial interactions move toward some kind of strange attractor. The patterns in the distribution of values, preferences, imaginations, and expectations within an emerging social system are the initial conditions also responsible for the future differentiation of the social aggregate, and these initial conditions represent the basin of attraction (Arrow and Burns, 2004).

The pattern in the distribution of values, preferences, imaginations, and expectations, called the basin of attraction, permeates also through the particular social field (Bourdieu, 1977). Because of the patterned basin of attraction, individuals do not live in a completely unpredictable environment. Field-specific rules enable individuals to anticipate and predict future tendencies and opportunities with certain probabilities. It is the way of decreasing uncertainty for individuals acting within particular social fields. Although the initial stages of cultural existence are typical by a relatively high uncertainty shared by the members of a culture, the so-called initial collective uncertainty, this uncertainty is gradually lowered as the shared system of field-specific rules becomes formed. This does not mean that from this time, the stability of a system is guaranteed, but we can at least say that safety-protecting mechanisms have been developed in a system.

It is necessary to emphasize that the qualities of a culture are not the simple sum of thoughts and behaviors of the individuals acting in the social field. There are also emergent properties that we are not able to extrapolate from the individual actions. Such emergent phenomena are often not possible to be explained using classic causality, i.e. as a linear relationship between some factor and its subsequent effect.

At this moment, it is also problematic to determine what kind of generalized, mathematically-derived strange attractor is responsible for the emergence or further development of particular social systems. This is an open field for further exploration and we may, therefore, posit:

OPEN QUESTION FOR FUTURE RESEARCH 1
What kind of strange attractors are responsible for the emergence and developments of social systems?

Let us turn our attention now to the dynamism and development of cultural elements in the time flux. Some of the established cultural norms and standards may become dominant in a given social system and some that are developed may become marginal. This also mirrors the types of memberships in social groups. Prototypical group members share the values, norms, and standards that are dominant in a given cultural system (Trnka, 2011), and they have a strong sense of group identity. On the other hand, peripheral group members may create their own social groups or subcultures with different values, norms, and standards (Trnka, 2011). Some of individuals may even become autonomous solitary within the cultural environment without adherence to any cultural values and norms.

It is necessary to say that sociocultural systems are perpetually moving and changing; they are in a constantly changing flux, i.e. in the process of flowing movement (Bohm, 1980). Despite this dynamic behavior, sociocultural systems show a historical continuity during their life cycle. For example, collective memory catches the continuity of a culture in the sense that each culture has its origin, development, and its end. Collective memory is the information structure of a culture that is different from the individual memories stored in the minds of individuals.

The continuity in the life cycles of sociocultural systems is in accordance with the character of transitions between the realm of potentiality and actuality. After each transition from the possible to the actual, the evolution of new tendencies and possibilities for future actualizations starts anew, but from a different starting point than before (Heisenberg, 1958; Schäfer, 2008). Schäfer (2008) suggested a continuous flux from the evolution of tendencies to their actualizations – empirical events – and from empirical events to new tendencies. Thus, the historical context of a culture is always essential for its further development.

As mentioned above, the emergence of man, groups, and cultures is governed by some kind of strange attractor. Chaotic behavior in these nonlinear quantum systems never settles into a predictable pattern in a long-term perspective (Judge, 1993). Periods of stability are always temporary and never permanent. The structures of sociocultural systems begin to break up as soon as they are formed (Judge, 1993). Thus, sociocultural systems are dynamic and highly unpredictable systems that are perpetually changing. Perhaps this is the reason why their investigation is so attractive for contemporary anthropologists...

Chapter 5
Fields, Groups, Cultures, and Social Complexity

Defining culture and social complexity in its entirety is an impossible task for only one book chapter. The question is if culture and social aggregates should really be even defined in any manner? The influences of postmodernism in the anthropological discourse of the eighties and nineties of the past century turned the attention of many anthropologists to the deconstructions of existing definitions rather than to the definition of the areas of social complexity. In the extreme instance, one may even adopt the position that nothing in the sociocultural reality can be possibly defined. This may seem to be a slightly problematic situation because with such an attitude, we would also refuse the fact that all anthropologists perceive and interpret the sociocultural reality in some way. Without a doubt, subjectivity is always present in anthropological investigation. Yet we hope that the reader may agree with the notion that most anthropologists are cognitively working with some kind of concept, and that at least some of them are able to name these concepts with such labels as social field, ethnic group, or subculture.

We are aware that the proper definition of culture and social groups perhaps transcends the limited possibilities of human analytical abilities and scientific writings. Something will always be omitted; something will always be missing. Keeping in mind our limited abilities to exhaustively explore the entirety of sociocultural reality, one should be aware of the reductionism of the efforts to provide complex definitions of culture or society. The definition we provide below also shares this limitation. However, we consider it to be an essential starting point serving to orient the reader in what we will be discussing throughout the book.

We start with the very nature of the relationship between culture and society itself. We argue that culture and society are entangled phenomena, and that they are therefore not two separable phenomena, but only one. Culture and society interact in the perpetual process of entangled mutual construction. Ingold (2005a) also pointed out such process-oriented mutuality of culture and society:

> "... cultural form ... is perpetually under construction within the context of people's practical engagements with one another. All culture, then, is social, in that its constituent meanings are drawn from the relational contexts of such mutual involvement; conversely all social life is cultural, since people's relationships with one another are informed by meaning ... culture and social life appear to be caught in an ongoing dialectic in which each ... 'constitutes' the other, through the mediation of human agency."
> (Ingold, 2005a, p. 738)

At the same time, however, this does not mean that anthropologists are not able to distinguish between culture and social aggregate. Although entangled, both phenomena have their own characteristic appearance. For better analytical purposes, we introduce here the concept of the macro-phenomenon that we call the "sociocultural meta-system". In this chapter, we will move step by step with the aim to define the sociocultural meta-system and its various appearances. We understand the sociocultural meta-system in a broader sense than, for example, Thompson (2000) who placed the focus only on the domain of educational research. In our understanding, the sociocultural meta-system is an all-encompassing complex that covers both social and cultural totality. It is the overall sociocultural reality, and various forms of observations may bring different insights on it based on the apparatus used. The sociocultural meta-system may be analyzed from various levels of analysis, and therefore different scientific disciplines have also developed specific expressions capturing the particular manifestations, such as individual mind, collective emotions, agency, or collective consciousness. Indeed, some terms used within the various scientific perspectives can be understood as the optics of the particular discipline. For example, anthropologists say that they investigate ethnic groups, subcultures, or national cultures; sociologists speak about societies, and psychologists about social groups, collective emotions, or collective unconscious. All of these perspectives explore the different particularities of the same psychosociocultural reality using various optics, methods, and levels of analysis. In the integral quantum anthropology introduced here, we do not wish to question the relevance of the outcomes of these particular scientific fields. Honestly, we respect the efforts of researchers in all areas. A pluralistic approach that we prefer to utilize is in line with the relativistic logic considered in the Introduction of this book.

In the following paragraphs, we introduce various cases of how the sociocultural meta-system may appear to researchers. When we speak about social systems or about cultural systems, we mean the different appearances of the sociocultural meta-system, i.e. "what appears to researchers". The nature of these appearances is always relativistic, depending on the methods and perspective used for investigations. Similarly, the exact boundaries of these systems do not really exist, but are only constructed by researchers within their fields. We believe that both the relativistic and the constructivistic logic can be applied when thinking about society and culture within the quantum anthropological perspective introduced by this book. Therefore, social and cultural systems are not understood in the closed and strongly restricted sense, but mostly as an analytical lens that provides us with the particular appearances of the sociocultural meta-system.

One of possibilities of what an anthropologist may explore is the appearance of the sociocultural meta-system in some form of social system. Although social anthropologists are engaged in the analysis of various forms of social organization, socialization, gender relations, and intergroup conflicts, they rather avoid the definition or specification of what a social system is. However, the complexity of sociocultural phenomena has forced us to introduce at least the rough outline of social system before proceeding further. The quantum anthropological perspective understands individual human beings as the basic elements of social systems, which perpetually interact and create, maintain, or untangle mutual social bonds. Interactions in the social system are suggested to behave similarly as the perpetually interacting microparticles in quantum systems. Thus, social bonds in social systems are perpetually changing in the sense of the ongoing reconfiguration of their structure. Quantum anthropology considers a social system to be a nonlinear, highly complex quantum system composed of the temporary interrelationships between its elements, i.e. individuals and groups. The delineation of a social system is always strongly influenced by the observer effect, e.g. the methods and perspective used for the investigation of the social system.

What are the examples of social systems? Various kinds of social systems or social aggregates have been investigated by generations of social and cultural anthropologists. Anthropological concerns consist of focuses on ethnic groups, subcultures, family systems, interest groups, or various kinds of communities, for example. Another form of social system may be distinguished as social systems that are defined by membership to national states. Aside from these, we can also observe virtual communities that may not be based on real face-to-face social interactions and physical social encounters. This is the case of virtual online communities that are based on communicating through the internet and online social networks.

Everything in a social system is relative and in the process of permanent change in time and space. A social system has an emergent nature, and its behavior cannot be understood solely from the knowledge of the actions of individuals, although individuals are the basic elements of it. All people are quantum beings, and our mutual interactions necessarily have quantum aspects (Wendt, 2006). The mutual interconnectedness between individuals and groups is analogical to the phenomenon known as entanglement in quantum mechanics. Particles/individuals exist only as a part of the macro-system in its entirety and are never isolated.

Generally, it might be posited that a social system is tightly linked with institutions like political institutions, legal institutions, religious institutions, leisure institutions, and any other organizational forms that are embedded in the cultural system that the given social system is entangled with. Sharing beliefs in common values or sharing spiritual or philosophical beliefs is suggested to be a source of the coherence of communities and various kinds of groups. But this sharing does not have to be found in all kinds of communities. Sharing political and legal institutions may be observed in social systems on the level of national states, but may be missing in subcultural or on-line communities, for example.

One of important questions is: how could the boundaries of social systems be defined? A possible answer is: This is impossible, because such defining is, in itself, a construction, and may thus deform the observed social reality. Therefore, it is reasonable to assume the idea of relative boundaries that are not fixed as in the case of the boundaries of national states. We argue that boundaries may be understood as fluid and unstable, depending on the way a social system is constructed. Social systems are constructed based on specific practices like linguistic, scientific and discursive acts (Barad, 2007). These acts have their specific agencies and modes of observation. Therefore, the specific configuration and nature of the apparatus by which the social system is observed is responsible for the construction of the boundaries and the persistence of their appearance over time.

The classic dichotomy of the emic versus the etic perspective may be used for illustration of two different ways that the boundaries of social systems may be constructed. The etic perspective denotes the view of observer and its "external" construction of a social system, whereas the emic perspective is much more based on the actions of social actors themselves, or more specifically, on their own formation of ethnic groups, subcultural groups, etc. The etic perspective is significantly shaped by modes of observations in anthropological research – these are processes of constructions, e.g. the scientific methods that are responsible for defining the boundaries of a social system.

In the case of the emic construction of a social system, the thoughts and actions of social actors play a role similar to that of the perpetually vibrating microparticles in a quantum system. Based on historical continuity, the thoughts of individuals, and their social actions, a social system is perpetually self-constructed in terms of autopoietical reproduction and self-organization (Luhmann, 1995). For an external observer, the thoughts and actions responsible for defining the boundaries of a social system appear to be internal processes of the system itself.

The emic construction of a social system is dynamic and perpetual. From this view, social systems are perpetually changing in the process of intra-active becoming, or the ongoing reconfiguration of boundaries (Barad, 2007). Their life trajectories begin when they emerge and end when they collapse. Various forms of possible developments are also the main topic of one of the following chapters.

As mentioned above, boundaries are supposed to be products of linguistic and discursive acts (Barad, 2007). Therefore, adopting social unit-related identity is a key process in the emic construction of social systems (Barth, 1969). Ethnic identity or subcultural identity are examples of such social unit-related identities. By the adoption and acceptance of these identities, membership in the social system is approved and individuals identify themselves with the social system.

Another question is the permeability of the boundaries of social systems. Social systems are not closed nor without any interactions with their environments. On the contrary, social systems have permeable boundaries, and ideas or communication flows may flow over them (Arrow and Burns, 2004). The external observer may identify these cross-border processes as the inputs and outputs of the social system. The permeability of the boundaries of social systems may change over time, and it is also selective – boundaries may be more permeable for some kinds of inputs or outputs than for others (Luhman, 1995).

When turning our attention to culture, we should characterize the basic features of cultural systems first. We argue that a cultural system is an informational spectrum shared by some of members of a given social system. Ingold (2005b) speaks about a shared system of concepts or mental representations, established by convention and reproduced by traditional transmission. Human culture may be understood as the outcome of multifaceted interactions amongst the diversified material and nonmaterial elements (Sarkar, 2002). In a more detailed aspect, a cultural system consists of shared patterns and informational structures, i.e. shared ideas, rules and symbols. We may identify elements of a cultural system that relate to the cognitive domain, for example, shared thoughts, beliefs, assumptions, attitudes, preferences, values, standards and interpretations. Furthermore, there are also some elements of cultural systems related to the behavioral domain, such as shared behavioral rules, norms, social scripts, prototypical actions, normative patterns of behavior, customs, habits, practices, ceremonies, and rituals.

It would be confusing to understand culture as a simple sum of parts. Although we have discussed cultural elements above, we wish to point out that there are also emergent properties that cannot be considered cultural elements. Such types of properties may emerge without any causation. It is difficult to reveal them, and to label them by using concrete terms. Emergent properties make cultural investigation slightly blurred, but it is better to take them into account than to refuse their existence because of their problematic observability.

Cultural systems and social systems are quantum systems, and as quantum systems they show various levels of coherence. Hodgson (1991) proposed that the continued relatively stable appearance of macro-objects is caused by continually interacting particles of which they are composed. When applying this assumption to the case of social systems, we may seek the source of their coherent appearance in the perpetual interactions inside their social networks. Thus, the pattern of interaction may maintain coherence, but it may also disturb coherence under some circumstances. Some patterns of interaction may destabilize the social system and shift some parts of system into unstable states.

In the area of cultural elements, each of the elements of a cultural system has its relative stability over time (resilience to change) and strength (the probability that most of its members will share and accept this cultural standard). We can consider resilience and strength to be qualities of cultural elements that relate to the quantum coherence of cultural systems. As in the case of the boundaries of social systems, it is also very difficult to define what exactly one cultural element is and what another one is. Cultural elements have plenty of mutual bonds, and it is suggested that they are strongly entangled. Therefore, the differentiation between them is considered to be a product of the analytical efforts of researchers rather than the case of objective, sharp boundaries.

The elements of a cultural system have various functions. For example, symbol systems and language are patterned symbolic structures that facilitate smooth semantic understanding between the members of a given culture. Aside from this, some of the cultural elements also influence the preestablished patterns that members of a culture can utilize as models for their behaviors. It is considered that the potentiality of human action may be actualized in time and space with certain probability. This potentiality covers both patterns for individuals and patterns for group behavior. Individual patterns are represented as behavioral rules, standards for actions, social interaction scripts, customs, norms for moral judgment, etc. Patterns meeting rather on the group level are sequences of collective actions, like social exchange and economics, various models for distribution, or scripts for collective decision-making (Arrow and Burns, 2004).

Culture may manifest itself in various forms. Manifestations of culture are actualizations of potentiality in time and space. Some of the pre-existing possibilities are actualized and some are not. Manifestations of a culture have a key significance for anthropology because manifestations are more readily available to our senses and perception, and therefore represent empirical material for anthropological analysis and interpretations. Some forms of manifestation have a material appearance (material culture), whereas others are observable through human action in the world (the behavioral domain of cultural manifestations). Material manifestations are those instances when culture manifests itself in some form of materialization that remains in various forms of relatively permanent matter, i.e. so-called material culture (i.e. Miller, 1998). Material manifestations consist of various forms of the arts, artifacts, practical tools, constructed environments, etc. Behavioral manifestations are very heterogeneous. Such instances are observable if culture manifests itself through human action without any material, relatively permanent output. Rituals, live music, dance, or some types of everyday human actions are examples of transient behavioral manifestations of cultural elements.

Interestingly, some manifestations of culture have a transitive nature, and it is very difficult to categorize them other than as transient or as permanent. For example, literature and human writings represent manifestations in both material and nonmaterial reality. Books are real material manifestations, but the stories that are included in them may be passed on by oral transmission. Digital texts found on the internet raise some questions. These are not an example of materialization, yet these texts are relatively permanent in time in comparison with a dance performance or a carried-out ritual, for example. The digital environment is virtual and has a very special character. It represents a very in-spiring issue for future discussions.

Let us turn our attention to the relation between culture and the agency of the members of a social system. Culture influences its members and members of a culture influence the culture ret-rospectively. Thus, there are generally two opposite directions of influences, top-down transmission and bottom-up change:

> *"Newcomers conform to group norms by observing and copying regularities in the way other members behave, and in this process we see the classic top-down transmission of culture from a higher level (the group) to a lower level (individual). Dynamic instabilities at the local level of a complex system can also create spontaneous change even after the system appears to have 'settled' into a persistent structure. ... This is bottom-up change."*
> (Arrow and Burns, 2004, p. 181)

The situation is more complicated when considering that each social system may, but also may not be linked to just one single cultural system. Indeed, a social system may be linked with one cultural system that most its members share, but some members may also accept elements of other cultural systems. It is also in-conceivable that a social system of, for example, national states is internally unsegmented. Internal alterity in the social system of-ten creates distinctive subcultural social systems with specific cul-tural norms and values that often differ from dominant cultural norms and values (Arrow and Burns, 2004). Barth (1969) speaks about the subdivision and multiplication of units. Music subcul-tures, alternatives, marginal ethnic groups, or marginal religious groups are examples of such subdivisions of social systems.

As we have argued above, a cultural system is an information-al spectrum shared by elements of a given social system. We un-derstand information as Weiner does (1961), that it is merely in-formation, not energy or matter. Bateson (1972, p. XXV–XXVI) defines information as *"the difference that makes a difference"*, it means something *"which changes us"*. And furthermore, informa-tion is also considered to be a "function of the observer" (von Foerster, 1988 [1973]), which is important to keep in mind when we speak about culture as a form of informational spectrum.

In a quantum world, particles are sensitive to gradients of information, as was proven in particle interference experiments

(Davisson and Germer, 1927). According to Schäffer (2006), in our ordinary world, our mind is the only thing (as we know) that can react to the flow of information. Social interactions and communication between individuals and various groups maintain information transfer and interference among the elements of a social system. What is more important, however, is that this social interaction also includes energies, i.e. emotional arousal.

Social interactions between individuals and various groups are constitutive forces of the dynamics of each social system. Most social interactions involve some kind of emotional arousal, and it is the emotional content itself that represents the energetic dimension of a social system. The exchange of emotional energies between individuals and groups on one hand and information exchange on the other causes a social system to have the characteristics of an energy-information field. Emotional energies or emotional arousal emerge during the course of interactions, and they further constitute interpersonal, intergroup, and interinstitutional relationships, e.g. the perpetual definition of ethnic or subcultural group boundaries, the identification of group membership, etc. For example, a shared fear of aliens helps to create bonds among members of the group, strengthen the group boundaries, increase willingness to fight for group values, reinvent roots (historical, literal, etc.) of the social or ethnic group, etc.

The emotional arousal of individuals is often entangled, because they are the functional elements of a quantum system. In such cases, the entanglement of emotional energies is observable as collective emotions, for example, mass panic, collective hysteria, or collective fears. Under these circumstances, the entanglement of emotional energies creates a "group mind" that is one of the forms of manifestation of collective consciousness (Wegner, 1987). Unlike other forms, it is possible to empirically observe and analyze this form of manifestation of collective consciousness.

Emotional arousal often happens through a trigger, which appears through one of our senses. Thus, for example, arousal can happen through touch (a punch, a kiss, or a caress), vision (seeing something shocking or desirable), hearing (a sudden noise, somebody saying something, music), smell (an evocative odor that triggers powerful memories), or taste (of wonderful or disgusting food). Emotions with an overpowering intensity stimulate people to act, often also in a non-rational way (Berger, 2011).

States of arousal can be positively or negative valenced, but it is not currently clear how many dimensions is optimal for the adequate description of subjective emotional experience (Trnka, 2013; Trnka et al., 2016). Our previous empirical study (Trnka et al., 2016) provided evidence that the use of several general dimensions for the measurement of subjective emotional experience is reductionistic. We argue that subjective emotional experience is multidimensional (Trnka, 2013; Trnka et al., 2016), and also that the quality of experience in terms of the number of experiential dimensions may vary according to the specific relational and situational configuration, i.e. the context. The current theory of multidimensional emotional experience (Trnka, 2013) works with this kind of logic and also elicits some similarities with the idea of Hilbert space. In the Hilbert space, it is possible to think of any finite or infinite number of dimensions. Similarly, for subjective experience, any number of experiential dimensions can be theoretically hypothesized. This parallel is preliminary and, therefore, we posit a future question:

OPEN QUESTION FOR FUTURE RESEARCH 2
Does man's subjective experience have the character of the Hilbert space?

Emotions can be also transmitted from one person to another person or persons. Emotional transfer is possible through the processes called affective resonance (Mühlhoff, 2015), or emotional contagion (Hatfield et al., 1994). These processes enable the collective sharing of emotions and we may even think about the possibility that affective resonance and emotional contagion are observable expressions of the quantum entanglement of emotional energies between people (compare with Mühlhoff, 2015).

Emotions have energetic qualities and influence the behavior of man within both the individual and the collective perspective. It is difficult to measure emotions empirically, but we may consider a hypothetical possibility that emotions, as energies, have their specific frequency (similarly as electricity, light, or nuclear energy). There are individuals that are more inclined to emotional "infections", and then there are individuals who are rather strong emitters of emotional feelings – they are charismatic individuals (Bhullar, 2012; Hatfield et al., 1994; Neumann and Strack, 2000). Thus, a charismatic person emits particular emotional frequency very strongly and becomes a sort of attractor for others, who, in turn, become attracted to this person. This is evident in many cultural and social activities. Participants of rituals, of pop concerts, or of a demonstration or speech of a political leader may share an emotional arousal and the same frequency of emotional energy. They experience a deep-rooted feeling of sharing and solidarity that fortifies the boundaries of the group, as well as their mutual bonds. People who share the same emotional vibrations (they are on the same wavelength) have stronger bonds between them. The same is applicable in physics – particles that have the same vibrations are mutually attracted to each other.

Short-term emotional arousal is used, for example, in shamanic rituals primarily focused on healing a sick individual. Some African tribes even use rhythmic group dancing – vibrations – to renew the rhythm (frequency) of the entire group (Penniman, 2002). Repeating these short-term experiences of shared emotional arousal leads to a continuous maintenance of the whole sociocultural system.

The Dayak Benuaq people investigated in our field research upheld their group boundaries and its continuity through specific funeral rituals (Figure 4). Traditional dual funerals are a characteristic mark of the Benuaq identity. To be a proper member of Benuaq society, one must properly organize this ritual. No matter how devote a Muslim or Christian the Benuaq was in life, very probably they shall desire this traditional animistic ritual at the end of their life's journey, so that they and their families may confirm and strengthen their group solidarity, including with their group of forebears (Lorencova, 2008). Schiller (1997) noted a similar trend with the Ngadju people of Borneo. Bacigalupo (1998) describes a similar process with the Mapuche in Latin America. Similar processes are described by the research of other anthropologists in other ethnic groups all around the world.

Emotional arousal, however, does not necessarily have to be shared only by individuals that personally know each other or are (physically) present together in one place, as is generally the case in rituals. The presently often-discussed issue of collective

Figure 4. Dayak women dancing *ngerankau* during *kuangkai,* the second funeral ritual, Damai, East Kalimantan, 2005 (Photo: Radmila Lorencová)

fear, which basically applies to all of western civilization, is an example of a "transnationally" shared collective emotion. The emotions of collective fear are not transmitted from one detectable center, nor are the individuals sharing this emotion in any acute danger. On the contrary, they emerge as waves from the energy-information field of collective consciousness or unconscious. In this case, these strong emotions are evoked by the fear of death encoded in each living being (we reflexively try to avoid death). Despite of the fact that there is a very small chance that the individual in question is actually in danger, they are exposed to conscious and unconscious triggers of fear thanks to the continuous repetition of media news containing key words such as terrorist, crisis, disaster, etc.

The emotional energy (vibrations) of individuals and groups spreads through space and time. Vibrations of a similar character evoked by individuals are mutually strengthened. Although the individuals do not mutually know each other nor do they see each other, they share the same emotional arousal on the basis of the informational interference.

As philosopher Bertrand Russel (2009) pointedly noted in his *Unpopular Essays* written already at the beginning of the last century, "Collective fear stimulates herd instinct, and tends to produce ferocity toward those who are not regarded as members of the herd". On one hand, then, fear strengthen the bonds among the members of a society (even though they do no know each other), on the other hand, it produces a mistrust among them and enables the auto-destabilization of the whole system. The situation of mistrust in the elements of the system, whether they be people or institutions (e.g. the church, science, the political or economical system, etc.), is usually designated as a social crisis.

Just as an individual is not constantly in a state of intense emotional arousal, then not even society is constantly in a state of collective emotional arousal. Despite of this, however, the sharing of emotions, a sort of emotional solidarity, occurs constantly. In the case of long-term and less marked emotions, we usually designate them as moods, emotional atmosphere, or emotional climate (Harrison, 2004). For example, in the Czech Republic, there was a strong collective euphoria (enthusiasm, joy after the fall of the Communist regime) in the period after the Velvet Revolution of 1989 (Kuška et al., 2013). After several years of building the new system, a decrease in activities and interest came about, and so the intensity of positive collective emotions also decreased. Society gradually "sobered up" from being inebriated by positive emotions, and on the contrary, began to notice the deficiencies of the new system, which was especially apparent in the distrust of politicians (many of which were even the leaders of the Velvet Revolution itself). The term "bad mood" was coined in 1997 first in the media, and then in society itself, and it became widely used; it was ascribed to then-president Václav Havel, who used it to apply describe the current situation. The expression became so popular that it became a part of common discourse. The "bad mood" did not describe any unexpected or short-term emotional arousal, but a long-term emotional mood shared by most of the members of society.

Emotions are also closely related to beliefs. These beliefs vary in different cultures and societies. A deep-rooted shared emotional energy can create such a strong belief that it can also change the everyday physical reality (e.g. through the ritual behavior that shall be discussed in more detail in Chapter 12). In the sociocultural meta-system, then, we find building blocks such as mass, information, and energy, which are also fundamental categories in quantum physics.

Clifford Geertz (1973) compared culture and its symbols to a web. We can also understand relationships between people as a web, as well as the organization of neurons in the brain. This is, however, only one part of reality as a whole, and the other parts are created by unobserved processes that take place within this web. The sociocultural meta-system carries in itself both elements that are observed and that are not observed. Observed elements are often the results of unobserved processes and the potentialities that occur in the nonempirical sphere. Just as matter emerges at the peak of colliding waves, then so do the elements of a cultural system become visible. The sociocultural meta-system is thus comprised of both potentialities and actualizations.

Chapter 6
Man as Embodiment

The understanding of man in quantum anthropology deserves special attention. Quantum mechanics has undermined the classic, Newtonian understanding of materiality, and since the human body is made of matter, it is legitimate to ask how such mattering can be understood? The quantum view of the world calls for a new definition of man within sociocultural anthropology. If man is a central object of anthropological inquiry, we should try to deconstruct the classic, Newtonian view of man.

Everyday concepts of the human body suggest that human bodies end at their skin, but currently, there are also efforts to relativize this classic view, especially within the "ontological turn" in sociocultural anthropology (e.g. Harris and Robb, 2012). For example, Barad (2007) has questioned the ambiguity of bodily boundaries. The identification of a concrete person is not suggested to be objective, but always influenced by sensing. The seemingly self-evident nature of bodily boundaries is, indeed, the result of specific actions of seeing, touching, etc. It implies that the identification of a concrete person thus depends on previous bodily engagements with the world, and on the repetition of culturally and historically specific bodily performance.

"... the body is always ontologically multimodal. In all societies, people understand it and experience it according to several sets of foundational principles that come into play in different circumstances and that sometimes exist in tension. These contexts are neither simply social nor material but, rather, always already both."
(Harris and Robb, 2012, p. 676)

On a more general level, material objects are not already there, but they emerge through specific practices (Barad, 2007). Thus, the human body is determined sensually, e.g. visually or tacti-cally. Based on the practices of seeing and touching, the given-ness of bodily boundaries appears to the observer; however, we can ask in earnest what is the human body? This is not the only question that arises. Another problem is the stability of matter over time. In the case of the human body, ongoing materializa-tion is present, and this process also calls for a deeper analysis of the quantum character of the human body. If our bodies are made of small energetic vortices, how are they emerging, how they are changing throughout life and how permanent and stable are these changes over time? These questions imply several possi-ble ways of deconstructing the traditional understanding of man based on the classic, Newtonian paradigm. We may start to think differently about the human being in the world. In this chapter, we will briefly touch on these types of issues, even though we feel that the quantum conception of man is still preliminary.

At the beginning we should ask how can the mattering of human bodies be understood? One possibility is to see man as a kind of embodiment. In contrast to the meaning of the term em-bodiment in Bourdieu's theory of practice (1977), the quantum anthropology of Russell (2013) understands embodiment as the actualization of potential and probability. According to this con-cept, man is seen to be an embodiment of a part of the energy-in-formation field. Russell (2013) uses the term "spirit" in the sense of a transcendental energy-information field or an essence of em-bodied reality. This labeling is, however, slightly problematic for a broader audience, because it may elicit the impression of some kind of esotericism. This is, however, solely given by the use of the term "spirit" (that is, nevertheless, commonly used within the discourse of theological anthropology). Indeed, the logic of anthropology of Russell (2013) is quantum-based, working with the distinction between the realm of potentiality and actuality. Energy-information is suggested to be transcendence, matter is embodiment. Energy-information essence is constantly present in the world, and a part of the energy-information field is hy-pothesized to manifest itself through matter, for example, in the form of a concrete person. This is, in fact, the act of embodiment.

Both the theory of practice (Bourdieu, 1977) and quantum anthropology (Russell, 2013) use the term embodiment, but with different meanings. In the theory of practice, embodiment is related to the process of acquisition of cultural capital by individuals, e.g. through learning. It is a feature of all cultures to have the potential of incorporating their cultural capital into their members. Just the process of embodiment is the fundametal process through which individuals may acquire cultural capital, it is also settled in their minds. In the theory of practice, the process of embodiment is understood much more as a metaphor of how culture influences the thinking of its members. On the contrary, in Russell's (2013) sense, embodiment is related to the matter. The human body is made of matter, and this manifestation of potentiality is a material form that also enables human action in the world. From this point of view, the material form, i.e. the human body, is a manifestation of a part of the overall energy-information potential (Trnka, 2015a). It is mattering that can be observed by human senses. Embodiment is suggested to be the basic aspect of human existence. Through embodiments, social actors can distinguish each other, and through embodiments, human interactions in the world are possible. A concrete person can be observed in certain time and certain place. It is thus one's own body that we consciously use for orientation in space. And, through our bodies, we create a representation about our body-world relation. In this sense, the body is suggested to be an initial point for human situatedness in the world.

We must be aware about this briefly-outlined distinction between Bourdieu's "cultural embodiment" (1977) and Russell's "embodiment from potentiality" (2013). We will work with Russell's quantum anthropological understanding of embodiment later in this chapter. Russell (2013) also discussed the issue of the limitedness of mattering. Matter is suggested to have the unlimited potential for the individual embodiments of energy-information potentiality. Both matter and energy-information essence are, although fundamentally different, interconnected always and everywhere; they are interfering constitutive moments of reality. This interacting is also a key dynamics for any transition between the realm of potentiality and actuality.

As mentioned above, the position of one's body is the basic point for the orientation of man in space. From this position, the body-world relation is perpetually constituted by our mental processes. The probability of choice and one's ensuing actions, which becomes definite, is also one's actual position in space and time (Russell, 2013). Without the knowledge of a person's position in space and time, one cannot say anything specific about his/her past or future behavior. In the case of humans, each embodiment is unique, and a certain level of alterity is always present. It is practically impossible to find two people who are absolutely the same both physically and mentally. We can find two or more people with similar personalities or physical appearances, but the absolute sameness is not meaningful, because both the human body and mind are highly complex systems.

As mentioned in other chapters, the overall energy-information potential is, in reality, potentiality (possibility, or probability), which can, under certain circumstances, be actualized (embodied) in time and space. Analogically to the shape of wave function, this potential is infinite, and yet, in the case of a person, is limited by the constrained possibilities of our world. When a part of the overall energy-information potential is actualized, the observer can identify a specific anatomical form – that is, a particular human body. Thus, every person is determined by his/her bodily form, in other words, by the material expression of a particular embodiment. But, this determination is time-dependent, and the human body as well as the human mind may change in time.

Aside of the material expression of embodiment, the embodied part of the overall energy-information field also influences the human mind and mental properties. Wendt (2015) understands man as a macroscopic instantiation of quantum coherence. An individual is seen as a coherent whole with its own, autonomous activity, such as anatomy, physiological processes, behavior, perception, and will. But in contrast to this local manifestation of quantum coherence, the human mind may also operate non-locally in some cases. The human mind can transcend the human body by the extension of consciousness into some extra-dimensions under special conditions, as we have showed in previous chapters (e.g. when dreaming, in altered states of consciousness, etc.). So, despite of the fact that the actions of the human body are always local, the human mind may also act non-locally under special conditions.

Human life can be understood as a series of collapses of the wave function. At the moment that any potentiality is being actualized (in the form of embodiment, for example), a collapse occurs in the same sense that a collapse of the wave function occurs (Russell, 2013). Every actualization or collapse automatically creates a new potentiality. After each collapse, a new palette of possibilities is created. The collapse of our wave functions is a perpetual process that proceeds continually as a person interacts with his/her internal and external environment (Wendt, 2006). The life of a person can be seen as a chain of collapses of wave functions, i.e. as observable flashes in time and space. This application of the collapse of wave functions in anthropology also has serious implications for the understanding of subjectivity:

> "... as an important part of our wave function, our knowledge of ourselves – our identity or sense of Self – does not have determinate properties at any given moment, but only becomes determinate when we act into the world (collapse). In other words, the desires and beliefs which the rationalist model of man sees as causing behavior actually do not exist until behavior takes place – before that point the Self is a superposition of multiple and mutually incompatible desires and beliefs. This does not mean identities are completely open-ended (in which case they wouldn't be 'identities'). Wave functions are highly structured sets of possible and probable states, making some behaviors and thus identities more likely than others. But these identities only become actualized in wave function collapse, which itself is undetermined by a physical process."
> (Wendt, 2006, p. 28)

Such thrownness of man in the world (Heidegger, 1996) also opens the question of free will and the possibility to make free decisions about future actions. The difference between the behavior of an electron and of a human lies in the fact that an electron cannot "choose" its position as a person can choose an action (Russell, 2013). The position of a particle at the moment of measurement is random. Man, however, acts consciously and actualizes various potentialities in space and time on the basis of their free will, and thereby attains a desired state on the basis of their own intentions. Human action is fundamentally anticipatory in the sense that in intentional action, we "feel" the future through a kind of temporal non-locality (Wendt, 2006). At the moment when man actualizes one of the potential possibilities of their life, all other potential possibilities collapse into one specific, embodied act in the continuous action or "coming into being" in space and time (Russell, 2013).

Man is not a mere, defenseless puppet strung along by fate. On the contrary, we are what we are thanks to our daily choices and actions. Man is an active instigator of reality, and thus actualizes their potentiality. People have relative freedom in their self-actualization, in their so-called transcendental freedom (Russell, 2013). This transcendental freedom is, however, always actualized through choices and actions in time and space. Such actualizations are known as categorical freedom.

Every person as an embodiment of the part of the overall energy-information field (Trnka, 2015a) does have an infinite number of potential choices; however, not every possibility in our life has the same probability of really occurring. It is our own personal history, our past actions, and decisions that, among other factors, shape and also limit our infinite potential so that some trajectories of our next development are highly probable, whereas others are highly improbable. The moment of the present is actually an interaction between our pasts and our futures.

Free will is, however, limited by social entanglement within our social networks. One is never alone in the world, and because of this, one's freedom is also limited. Free will is never absolute. On the contrary, we are all a part of interconnected interpersonal agencies, others' interests, public interests, the interests of politicians on the national and international level, etc. (Trnka, 2015a). The mutual interdependence between interfering agencies, interests, and motivations is analogical to the phenomenon known as entanglement in quantum mechanics. Both particles and people exist only as a part of the macro-system in its entirety and are never isolated. Every free human action has the potential to develop, to qualitatively change, or to limit the sphere of freedom of someone else or of an entire group of people. Free will is thus always restricted.

Aside from the interests of others, every person is also embedded into a certain situation and certain context. Situations and contexts may be historical, cultural, ethnic, sociopolitical, etc. This contextual embeddedness mirrors the quantum logic, again especially in the realm of quantum entanglement. The action of every man is entangled within the local as well as the non-local networks of interests. These interests are agentic and influence the decisions about future actions of man. We can assume that, thanks to the internet and to the development of telecommunication technologies, this entanglement is on the rise in today's globalized world.

The existence of man has been defined as an embodiment of a part of the energy-information field. A problem arises, however, when we turn our attention to cultures and societies. When analyzing cultures, subcultures, ethnic groups, or communities, it is questionable if we may also speak about embodiments. Cultures and various social units exist in time and space, but they cannot be observed as material entities. They are manifestations of overall energy-information potential, but these manifestations are often nonmaterial.

However, we can observe the expressions of cultural elements. Culture may manifest itself through human action in the world. Within the behavioral domain, we can observe transient forms such as rituals or dance. In contrast, material manifestations, such as the arts, artifacts, technology, or constructed environments are relatively stable over time. It is important to realize that all forms of the material embodiments of a cultural system are indeed the productions of this very system. We argue that culture is productive, and that cultural productivity is one of main agentic features of each culture. Cultural systems produce material entities or transient behavioral manifestations through the human action in the world. Again, however, cultural productivity is possible only because of human action in the world, and at the same time, human action is possible only through and by human bodies. This is the quantum entanglement between the realm of potentiality, embodiments, and the expression of potentiality in the observable world.

As seen above, some parts of cultural system may be manifested through human activity in the material world, but we cannot observe the culture itself. Culture in its entirety is invisible. We can observe only its material products or the outputs manifested in human behavior or actions. These appearances are also available to the observer, e.g. in our case, an anthropologist. An anthropologist cannot see a culture directly, he/she is only dependent on those expressions of culture that manifest to his/her sensual apparatus. This selective and indirect access to culture makes each anthropological investigation limited. We always may observe and analyze only some events, actions, or images. The underlying cultural forces remain hidden at least in part.

(79)

So, it is suggested that it is not possible that the overall complexity would be revealed in a single anthropological investigation. Instead, the continuity in anthropological inquiry creates a more reliable picture about sociocultural phenomena. More views, more perspectives, and more interpretations may help overcome the burden of subjectivity in anthropological research. And again, the key importance of the complementarity principle (Bohr, 1928) for sociocultural anthropology is apparent here.

We can conclude that, on the general level, man and culture both share the character of the actualization of potential possibilities in time and space. Similarly, ethnic groups, subcultures or various communities are the temporal constellations of social relations that have been actualized from the overall pool of possibilities. From this point of view, man, cultures, and social units share the similar characteristics of actualization in time and space. Both cultures and social units exist, at least in our minds, but the difference is that the appearance of man shows a higher material coherence than that of cultures and social units. Whereas man is a material whole with their own anatomy, physiology, and sensory qualities, cultures and social units do not have such a degree of materialization. Both cultures and social groups also show quantum coherence over time, but their coherence is virtual, and it is not possible to observe it directly using our senses. We can observe the behavior of people or of their products, but not the cultures themselves.

Thus, cultures, ethnic groups, subcultures or various communities are actualizations, but not embodiments in a material sense. Therefore, our knowledge about cultural elements is always vicarious and not direct. This should not be frustrating for us, but this difference should be kept in mind when conducting any anthropological investigation focusing on culture or social life. On the other hand, the same limitation is true also for a big part of psychological research. Cognition, reasoning, or motivation are also nonmaterial phenomena and they cannot be measured directly. Such impossibility brings some limitations to a deeper understanding of social and cultural phenomena. However, we should like to end this chapter with the optimistic claim that this limitation should be accepted as a stimulating incentive rather than as some trap of hopelessness.

Chapter 7
Collective Consciousness
and Collective Unconscious
in Anthropology

The beginning of the new millennium was marked by a massive wave of studies focused on human consciousness. Many researchers have been fascinated by various quantum explanations of human consciousness, and these interests have spread across different disciplines. This field, which was previously considered to be problematic and often shifted into the area of things that are "not possible to be investigated", has started to become one of the most quickly accelerating scientific fields. More importantly, this common interest has also unified researchers from philosophy, psychology, anthropology, and neuroscience in their efforts to interconnect individual consciousness, collective consciousness, culture, and collective agency. These efforts have gone across different scientific fields and approached human consciousness on various levels of analysis.

Currently, the research and theory in the field of quantum consciousness is so extensive that it is above the capabilities of one book chapter to summarize all of the main areas (but see e.g. Atmanspacher, 2004; Mensky, 2010; Rosenblum and Kuttner, 2006). For the purpose of building a new quantum anthropology, we have selected only some areas that will be briefly touched upon later in this chapter. We aim to especially introduce the collective level of consciousness, because it is closely related to human culture, agency, collective action, and collective behavior. Furthermore, we will also briefly outline the main features of collective unconscious because of its relationship with ritual practices and myth.

A strong wave of interest about human consciousness has emerged in current sociocultural anthropology, but the understanding of collective consciousness is slightly fluid and unanchored at this time. Aside from issues like historical consciousness, historicity, or collective memory, there are also current anthropological concerns focusing on religious life, transcendence, and rituals. For example, in the study of Holmberg (2006), consciousness is discussed in relation to the production of magical or symbolic power and to the processes of transcendence. Here, attention was focused on the way rituals seek to transform affected subjects into active agents. The processes of symbolic transcendence are suggested to be possible through ritual practices. During the ritual, and through the shamans' transcendent moves, social orders are deconstructed, and through the exposition to the constructedness or the arbitrariness of those orders, the affected subjects are stirred to agential states both individually and collectively.

The study of Bacigalupo (2014) focuses on the way oral shamanic biographies and performances contribute to the formation of historical collective consciousness. By textualizing shamanic power in the form of "bibles", shamanic literacies may speak to a broader audience and play, therefore, a central role in the production of the historical collective consciousness. The process of textualizing itself is considered to contribute to shamanic rebirth.

Roberts (2012) has different interpretative insights, and turns his attention to the dynamics of collective consciousness in time, and especially to the production of secular truths about religion by colonial forces. This work links the field of collective consciousness with the framework of postcolonialism and postcolonial studies. The native collective consciousness is supposed to be shaped by the power of colonialism, and conversion to other than native religion is understood as a type of conquest. The author calls this process a "colonization of consciousness" or "mental colonization".

All of the aforementioned interesting anthropological works direct our attention to the fundamental question of what human collective consciousness really is? As is apparent from the nature of this field, this question cannot be answered simply. Vice versa, some ambiguous answers can be expected. There is currently a high number of different definitions and explanations of the phenomenon of collective consciousness. Some of these explanations have mutual contact surfaces and some do not. We do not dare choose or reject any of the explanations here. The discussion in the discourse of consciousness research is actually so tempestuous that it indicates the mainstream opinion is still in the process of formation. Therefore, we will adopt the pluralistic approach, and shall introduce the main explanations seeking the nature of collective consciousness in the following section.

Ideas about the nature of consciousness have some principles in common. Generally, collective consciousness is not idealized as separate units of entities, but rather as a field. When we think about human collective consciousness, we probably think about some kind of quantum field, because of the quantum nature of the deep microstructure of our world. It is too early to try to provide the detailed characteristion of such a field here. A field may be generally conceptualized as a space in which interactions occur (Combs and Krippner, 2008), but the character of it is still unknown. Aside from Durkheim's classic original meaning (1997 [1893]) and from Murphy's (1945) theory of an interpersonal fields, there are currently several hypotheses in question. We may consider Roll's (1965) psi field theory, Laszlo's (1995) cosmic plenum, Eccles' (1994) quantum level synaptic events, Grandpierre's (1997) collective biological fields, Hameroff and Penrose's (1996) fields composed of entangled vibrations of neural microtubules, or Combs and Krippner's (2008) resonance of micro-level dendritic and synaptic fields of separate nervous systems. This high variability of explanations mirrors the complexity of this issue well.

Although no general acceptance of one of explanation's idea has been found in this field, most of the aforementioned theories suppose some kind of binding. Collective consciousness is suggested to be field that emerges based on some process of quantum binding (e.g. quantum entanglement). It is the extension of individual consciousness into a higher, collective level. During such quantum binding, the fields of individual consciousness transcend the borders of the organism and interfere with the consciousness of another person or persons. Maybe it is only a game with words, but the central idea is similar. Despite of the physical character of such quantum binding, it is suggested that conscious activities of individuals interfere and the field of collective consciousness then emerges based on this interference. This process has a character of coupling between the different-level processes called local-global coupling (Grandpierre, 1997). It is a kind of coupling between the local level of individual consciousness and the global level of collective consciousness.

We may imagine a type of connectivity between individual minds whose activities interfere and thus form the field of collective consciousness. For example, Combs and Krippner (2008) assumed the form of connectivity through subtle, very low levels of energy:

> *"What seems to be needed, at least as a starting point, is a way to understand how the brain can be responsive to patterns of stimulation carried by 'subtle', very low levels of energy. The importance of low energy stimulation of some type is suggested by the fact that experiences of collective consciousness seem to occur most often during alternative states of consciousness such as trance or sleep states, as would seem to be the case with the African San peoples and Australian Aborigines, or during a silencing of the ordinary chatter between individuals and within the individual mind."*
> (Combs and Krippner, 2008, p. 5)

This claim is also in accordance with Grandpierre (1997), who worked with the idea of collective consciousness as a kind of collective biological field. He hypothesized that human consciousness fields interact primarily at the α-level in frequencies around 7.5 Hz. Based on binding interactions and the resonance of consciousness fields, the field of collective consciousness emerges. Alpha-level interactions also support the idea of a subtle level of connectivity between the brains of individuals who share a particular field of collective consciousness. It is a kind of quantum entanglement that is supposed to be responsible for such invisible connection. Combs and Krippner (2008) explained connectivity by amplifying micro-level events in dendritic fields and near synapses into macro-level process. The process of amplifying micro-level events may be understood as the underlying substrate for the idea of the macro-level extension of the individual activities of consciousness into a higher level of activity of collective consciousness.

Given this mode of connectivity between individual minds, collective emotions may be experienced in individuals who interfere with a particular field of collective consciousness. The emotional arousal of individuals interacts within entangled collective consciousness, and collective emotions such as mass

(84)

panic, collective hysteria, or collective fears may occur due to induction effect (Grandpierre, 1997). Collective emotions can be experienced also during rituals or trance states, e.g. in collective dance parties.

Here, we can posit that the interference between individual minds can create a field that is of a different quality than the primary emotional arousal of individuals. We interpret this by quantum entanglement between individual minds in moments when collective emotions occur. The emotional arousal of individuals interferes under certain circumstances and creates a kind of a collective emotional arousal that is of different quality than the initial sum of initial individual arousal. Thus, quantum interference is proposed here as being responsible for the specific nature of collective emotions.

We argue that the experience of collective emotions is not of the same quality as the experience of collectively shared social identity. The "we feeling" or the "sense of us" may be present in some cultures, ethnic groups, or subcultures. Wendt (2015) considers the collective sharing of social identity in members of a group to be a group-level feeling. By the collective sharing of social identity, individuals may experience social unity or social belonging. It is a mode of relating to each other, or collective self-awareness. Wendt (2015) understands it as a social wave function that is present either in co-presence in a specific situation, or also non-locally by virtue of the entanglement of the "we feeling" between individuals. The collective sharing of social identity is also closely related to collective agency and to shared motivations involved in working towards a common goal.

The question is whether we may fathom a kind of quantum connectivity in the case of the collective sharing of social identity? During mass panic, collective hysteria, or trance states during rituals or dance parties, individuals are involved in sharing the special shared emotional arousal and genius loci of time and space. In the case of the collective sharing of social identity, we may consider a kind of opinion or belief transfer that may be motivated by previous socialization within a particular cultural or ethnic group. Therefore, it is questionable if we are speaking about comparable experiences. Individual opinions or beliefs do not necessarily require quantum entanglement, because we may imagine that information about social belonging can be transmitted via communication, e.g. from parents and group members to offspring and descendants. Thus, the "we feeling" may be a relatively strong emotion experienced in the consciousness of individuals, but such an emotion can be simply elicited by the minds of individuals who have fully accepted a group identity. So, although very important issue for anthropologists, we leave the question about the nature of the "we feeling" open to further investigation.

OPEN QUESTION FOR FUTURE RESEARCH 3
Can the experience of collective social identity require quantum interference within the field of collective consciousness?

Let us now turn our attention to the area that carries a seemingly similarly title, but is of a quite different nature, indeed. It is the realm of collective unconscious. On the general level, Wendt (2006) defines collective unconscious as the background knowledge we have and of which we are not aware when we are in normal states of consciousness. In Jung's tradition, Schäfer (2008) follows the definition of collective unconscious as a "psychic system of a collective, universal, and impersonal nature which is identical in all individuals and that consists of pre-existent forms, the archetypes, which can only become conscious secondarily". The Jungian collective unconscious is a system that is understood to be structured by a set of primary, unobservable, and irreducible elements called archetypes. Archetypes are suggested to be completely invisible and appear only symbolically in dreams, fantasies, and altered states of consciousness in the form of primordial archetypical images. It means that archetypes may be actualized in time and space in the form of primordial images through the mediation of human agency. We understand such instances to be a manifestation of the collective unconscious in empirical reality. Thus, the collective unconscious is a transcendental dimension of our reality common for all cultural groups, but the particular observable expressions of collective unconscious depend also on the cultural context and tradition.

"The structure of the collective unconscious is given by archetypes, whereas its content is given by the archetypical (or primordial) images, which never have an individual character but rather have a collective nature. The arche-

(86)

typical images are a type of 'historical precipitate' of the collective memory whose existence is suggested to us, inter alia, by the recurrent mythological themes that are likely common to every race and all epochs. The archetypes express themselves by means of symbols or images; they are the same for every person on the planet. ... Depending upon adaptation, the social environment, and enculturation, some archetypes develop, while others languish in a relatively undeveloped state; when archetypes develop into more elaborated structures, they are called complexes."
(Iurato, 2015, p. 64)

The main implication of the concept of collective unconscious for e.g. the theory of practice (Bourdieu, 1977) is that every mythology and archaic practice is peculiar to any human being of any time, and that such practices thus have an ahistorical and an atemporal structural nature, regardless of culture (Iurato, 2015). The collective unconscious is a primary source for mythology and religious symbolism. It informs an agent's actions and thoughts, especially in fields such as religion, the arts, etc. It is possible to approach the realm of the collective unconscious in dreams, in fantasies, and in altered states of consciousness, however, this unconscious source itself always remains to be outside of individual cognition.

In anthropology, the idea of collective unconscious is distinguishable in the structuralism of Lévi-Strauss (1963). Lévi-Strauss understands the structural unconscious to be the universal basis for every human thought of every epoch and every civilization, based on which the common laws of social systems emerge. The Lévi-Straussian unconscious is understood to be a metastructure categorized into pure free-content forms with a universal, atemporal, and formal character. It is something that can be called the universal mind. Such a universal mind is supposed to include the finite number of the possible variants of logic with which it operates. Only the common logic structures the realm of collective unconscious, and this logic may allow various symbolic thoughts to emerge. Thus, the collective unconscious is a source of the transindividual symbolic order. The Lévi-Straussian unconscious model works with the possibility of the transposition of every individual consciousness towards a higher plane. This idea is closely related to the concept of extension proposed by the quantum anthropology we are introducing here.

Iurato (2015) compares the Jungian and Lévi-Straussian understanding of collective unconscious. The main difference has been found in the appreciation of stability of content of the collective unconscious. The Jungian collective unconscious may undergo changes in terms of their dependence on the phylogenetic or cultural evolution. Thus, the collective unconscious is an objective structural entity conceived of as universal sediments of past experiences. In contrast, the Lévi-Straussian collective unconscious is primarily characterized by the absolute and full predetermination of its structural forms. Such elementary and irreducible structures are suggested to be of an omnitemporal nature, and they are supposed to be independent of the time flux.

The concept of archetypes as being the basic constituents of collective unconscious is interesting, but it also brings about several difficulties. For example, we do not know how archetypes come into being from the basic level of potentiality. In previous chapters, we argued that the emergence of any system must be based on some set of underlying zero states. Trnka (2015a) uses the term "overall, wave-particle energy-information potential", denoting an underlying all-pervasive substructure of zero states that provide energy-information potential for all actualizations in time and space. This concept supposes that the energetic properties of individual microparticles serve as a pre-existing source of information for future actualizations. In physics, Puthoff's (2002) quantum sea of zero-point fluctuations is a candidate for explaining the physical nature of the overall, wave-particle energy-information potential with which we work here. Simply stated, the constellation of qualities of microparticles in a vacuum, i.e. quantum vacuum energies, represents the underlying all-pervasive substructure of zero states for all future possible actualizations.

The idea of overall, wave-particle energy-information potential shares the same hypothetical foundation with the understanding of archetypes, because both are predicted to be a set of primary, unobservable, and irreducible elements. Yet they are not the same. On one hand, there are zero-point fluctuations as a random, fluctuating energies in the vacuum, and patterned, more complex elements called archetypes on the other. Both zero-point fluctuations and archetypes represent the realm of potentiality, but the complexities of these potentials are different. Thus, we argue that the vacuum energies of microparticles and archetypes are not of the same nature. Whereas microparticles in the vacuum are random energetic vortices, archetypes are some kind of patterns, or patterned structures.

If archetypes are more complex phenomena than zero-point fluctuations in the vacuum, it is not likely that the generation of archetypes precedes the potentiality of continuous virtual particle-pair creation and annihilation in the vacuum. We consider vacuum processes of the overall, wave-particle energy-information potential to truly be the primary substrate of the realm of potentiality. By and through patterning, archetypes are supposed to be formed from the initial quantum vacuum energies. Thus, archetypes are suggested to emerge secondarily, as a result of quantum patterning based on primary chaotic processes in the vacuum. We can theoretically compare the patterning of archetypes to some kind of intermediate state between the realm of initial potentiality, i.e. quantum vacuum energies, and the manifestation of archetypes in the world, i.e. primordial images.

This hypothetical prediction is preliminary, and we do not yet have sufficient evidence to support our idea now. Some interesting insights supporting the aforementioned idea of a hypothetical intermediate state are provided by Merrell (2009). Merrell's study is primarily focused on the general process of semiosis (Figure 5), not on patterning of archetypes, but we introduce

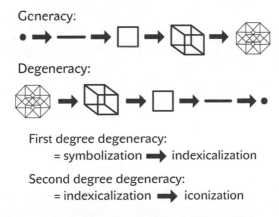

Generacy:

Degeneracy:

First degree degeneracy:
    = symbolization ➡ indexicalization
Second degree degeneracy:
    = indexicalization ➡ iconization

Figure 5. Sign generacy and degeneracy (Source: Merrell, 2009)

one of its ideas here since it may stimulate subsequent discussions. Merrell (2009) speaks about the general stage of prefiguring the sign in the process of semiosis. The sign is supposed to emerge out of "emptiness", "no-thingness", or, the zero state. However, there are two proposed instances of zero states, emptiness and empty set. Emptiness refers to a state that is absolutely empty; it is the possibility for the emergence of anything and everything – all objects, acts, practices, and events. There is no predicted straightforward relationship, however, from absolute emptiness to the manifestation of possibilities. On the contrary, some kind of intermediate state is hypothesized. Merrell (2009) calls it the empty set. The empty set denotes a mesophase between absolute emptiness and actualization in time and space. Empty set is the phase when a sign enters into the range of concrete possibilities. It is something like the "noticed absence" of something that was or could have been, or might possibly be there partially or wholly to fill the unoccupied space (Merrell, 2009). This suggested hypothetical intermediate state is not very easy to imagine, but we may speculate about some kind of analogy with the intermediate state in the process of archetype patterning predicted in this chapter. Empty set is a similar hypothetical instance of a state that is in between the primary source of potentiality and the actualization. More research is needed to clarify this issue. For future anthropological thinking, we may only postulate some key questions regarding the generation and patterning of archetypes.

OPEN QUESTION FOR FUTURE RESEARCH 4
What relationships do archetypes and initial, vacuum zero-point fluctuations have?

OPEN QUESTION FOR FUTURE RESEARCH 5
What role do strange attractors play in the quantum patterning of archetypes in the realm of potentiality?

Chapter 8
Life Trajectories of Man, Cultures and Societies

When investigating ethnic groups, subcultures, or national cultures, one can accept that such forms of social coherence have a certain durability in time. Cultures and social aggregates exist in time – they emerge, evolve, and collapse. Between the emergence and the final collapse, there is a period where the identity of these systems can be, at least to some extent, congruently recognized by external observers. And, during this period, both cultures and social aggregates are not static. In contrast, they are perpetually changing; in other words, they are in the process of flowing movement (Bohm, 1980). We can discuss processes, dynamics, chains of historical events, or the course of historical development. And the main aim of this chapter is to explore the variability in the dynamics and processes that can be found in the lives of man, cultures, and groups.

Time is just what enables cultures and social aggregates to change. The terms "flux" or "temporality" (Luhmann, 1995) describe the temporal qualities of cultures and social systems on the general level of analysis. Temporality is always relative, because it depends on the position of the observer who makes a judgment about the duration of entities over time. From the position of the observer, something may appear less durable than something else. When the perspective of observation is changed, however, the previous judgments may change, as well.

However, not all things are temporal. The converse of temporality is omnitemporality. This means that omnitemporal things are timeless, and as such are supposed to exist in cultural systems. Collective memory is an example of an omnitemporal structure. The memory of a system includes information acquired through the experiences of the system itself, which is then stored for repeated use in future. Such informational patterns are suggested to endure over time.

But, when we realize that it is actually us, anthropologists, who are the observers stating that collective memory is omnitemporal, we may relativize such a statement. The impression of omnitemporality might be only caused by the limited time scale that we are working with. For example, astrophysicists work within the time framework of billions of years, evolutionary anthropologists within the span of millions of years, and cultural anthropologists within the span of thousands of years. All of these scientists approach various phenomena within the temporalities of their disciplines. When accepting this relativity, we may ask if the collective memory of a culture would not appear to be omnitemporal only because of the working time scale?

OPEN QUESTION FOR FUTURE RESEARCH 6
Is collective memory omnitemporal or not?

The limits of anthropological inquiry should be taken into account when exploring the time dimension of the existence of cultures and groups. Anthropologists have limited sequences of frames of how sociocultural reality appears to their apparatus available. These sequences or "flow of frames" are just what inform the anthropologist about the dynamics of sociocultural reality in time. The alterity between frames in a time sequence is what creates the appearance of some kind of movement in the observed sociocultural reality. In the case that frames would be absolutely identical in some time period, it would be impossible to identify any kind of process or change. However, such a hypothetical case does not correspond with the many decades of experience of anthropologists with the observation of ethnic groups, subcultures, or national cultures in time. Despite of the relatively limited time span of sociocultural anthropology, we may accept that sociocultural reality is not stable over "longer" time periods. Changes and developments are almost always present, and thus, it is legitimate to speak about the processes, the social dynamics, and the time-dependent differentiation of cultures and social aggregates.

The investigation of social and cultural dynamics is very difficult, and we face several methodological problems. For example, at the beginning of this chapter, we proposed that the analysis of cultures or social aggregates requires at least some congruency in their identifications between researchers. The coherence of the human physical body is often relatively stable during the life of a person. However, the identification of culture as a coherent system is slightly problematic. We have already discussed in more detail the problem of boundaries in the chapter on the quantum view of culture and social life (Chapter 5). Thus, the exact boundaries of cultures are supposed to be problematic to delimit, as they are products of our constructions. Boundaries are fluid and unstable, based on the way a constructed cultural system is defined in time and space. In this situation, the life trajectories of cultures and social systems are difficult to trace as their boundaries are changing over time.

Another difficulty is that the development of cultural elements often varies because of the speed of changing. The speed of changes of the elements of a cultural system is closely related to the qualities of these cultural elements, such as relative stability over time or resilience against change. Some cultural elements are relatively stable over time, for example, language, customs, habits, ritual patterns, ceremonies, or traditions. In contrast, thoughts, beliefs, attitudes, preferences, and values are more susceptible to change and less stable over longer time segments. We consider these differences to be differences in the temporal qualities of cultural elements.

All of these limitations are important to realize and consider when reading the following sections, including the general analysis of the variability in the life trajectories of man, cultures and social aggregates. Before proceeding further, we should explore this issue in more detail. We leave the issue of the physical human body aside, because it is not so problematic from the viewpoint of coherence. As mentioned above, however, cultures have perpetually changing boundaries. So, how we can trace the development of the life trajectories of cultures and social systems?

In Chapter 5, we provided definitions of culture and social system. However, these definitions were rather static and provided us only with the initial set up of the field of our interest. It was just a simple description of the area. Here, however, we shift to the perspective of time. Now, we are working with the time and development of cultures and societies in the course of the time flux. And, therefore, we need to "change the optics".

Within the static definition, we defined culture to be composed of cultural elements like language, values, preferences, beliefs, ritual patterns, customs, or traditions. Culture is suggested to be composed of many of such elements, and therefore, it is undoubtedly a highly complex phenomenon. When we consider the time dimension, we should also change the view of the inner structure of culture. As mentioned above, some cultural elements are relatively stable over time and some are not. The speed of change varies in different cultural elements. It is important to realize that a particular cultural element is constructed at the moment of anthropological observation. This is only the moment in the time flux when an anthropologist observes a particular culture. Yet culture is a multidimensional complex, and its development cannot be described by one single trajectory, but it is reasonable to think about parallel developments within multiple dimensions. Therefore, we will not define the life trajectory of a culture as one simple dimension, but as a multidimensional complex of developments proceeding in parallel. We consider these parallel trajectories to be different ways in which culture is changing over time. In this sense, we introduce the term dimension of development here.

The dimensions of development are the routes in which culture or a social system flow. We should note again that cultural elements itself cannot be observed directly. Anthropological knowledge depends on the observation of manifestations of culture through people's action, testimonies, expressions, behaviors, and productions. Some of the dimensions of development are linked to cultural elements, but some dimensions are characterized by the process of change itself, and have not even been manifested in any (either directly or indirectly) observable phenomena. Such dimensions are supposed to be hidden to our observations, but are suggested to interfere with observable expressions. The unobservable dynamics are hypothesized to have the character of uncollapsed wave functions. These wave functions are suggested to be an underlying part of our nonempirical reality. It is important to say that in the case of cultures or social systems, their existence is only hypothetical, but we take this prediction into consideration based on the analogy with the behavior of quantum microparticles.

The main purpose of this chapter is to briefly outline the various ways that man, cultures, and societies may change during the course of their life trajectories. As mentioned above, man, cultures, and social groups as complex nonlinear systems are perpetually changing; they are in the constantly changing flux, i.e. in the process of flowing movement (Bohm, 1980). In these complex nonlinear systems, various forms of changes and processes may occur. Let us first introduce the general theoretical basis for the analysis of the variability of processes in cultures and social systems.

We argue that it is appropriate to analyze the dynamics of the development of man, cultures, and societies in time through the concept of homogeneous, heterogeneous, and neuterogeneous inner dynamics (Trnka, 2015b). This kind of thinking assumes the three dynamic principles that follow the general dialectic of the philosophy of G. W. F. Hegel (1770–1831). This dialectic assumes the conflict of two opposites and the existence of a third principle that reconciles the opposite agency of these two opposing forces. According to this principle, human history is understood as a constant process of dialectic clash (Yolles et al., 2008).

A similar logic has been also used in the conceptualization of homogeneous, heterogeneous, and neuterogeneous inner dynamics (Trnka, 2015b). The starting point was that the basis of any change in the social aggregate stems from the effect of the actions of two binary opposites. The following passage introduces how homogeneous, heterogeneous, and neuterogeneous inner dynamics work, and how they influence changing patterns in social aggregates.

Three general forms of inner dynamics are suggested to potentiate the processes in systems and affect the functioning of systems in a specific direction. They are not causal factors, but rather the inner characteristics of various developments and transitional states during the course of the life trajectories of nonlinear quantum systems. Homogeneous inner dynamics is generally characterized by an invariance and a tendency to return things to their original state of order, i.e. to the very beginning of their existence. Heterogeneous dynamics is, in contrast, a source of differentiation, diversity, and multiplicity. It is a primary source of alterity in the world. Heterogeneous inner dynamics stimulates change and the creation of various things, it stimulates production. It disrupts sameness.

In contrast and thirdly, a neuterogeneous inner dynamics maintains harmony, order, and basically serves to protect the existence and the stability of the system. It ensures an equilibrium between the homogeneous and the heterogeneous dynamics. Thus, neuterogeneous inner dynamics may be considered to be a preserver of life, i.e. it preserves quantum coherence in various existing systems.

As apparent from this general outline, the actuations of heterogeneous inner dynamics have an opposite force to that of homogeneous inner dynamics. The overgrow of homogeneous or heterogeneous inner dynamics causes the destabilization of system. If one or the other prevails too much, the system is destabilized and has the tendency to collapse. We may understand homogeneous and heterogeneous inner dynamics as two complementary, uncollapsed waves that are in a dialectic relationship. One dynamics actuates the processes that are opposite to the other dynamics. The homogeneous and heterogeneous complementary waves underlie the processes that are observed during the life trajectories of man, cultures and societies. Although complementary, absolute harmony between them is very rarely observed and is always only temporary. Further along in the text, we turn our attention to specific examples of instances where homogeneous and heterogeneous inner dynamics are suggested to potentiate various kinds of processes.

When thinking about real, observable situations and dimensions of development, we should first admit that various types of dynamics have their specific properties. The general definition of homogeneous, heterogeneous, and neuterogeneous inner dynamics may seem too vague to conjunct it with specific observed instances in anthropological research. Therefore, we aim to introduce here a preliminary categorization of processes with prevailing homogeneous, heterogeneous, or neuterogeneous inner dynamics. At the beginning, it is necessary to highlight that this typology is only preliminary, and we do not claim that this typology is exhaustive. We are far from maintaining this position. Rather, we aim to provide something that could be a starting point for follow-up discussions and developments. The typology provided here is not complete and should be elaborated and supplemented with new instances and examples in the future.

For the purpose of our current analysis we posit the following types of agentic states that also underlie various processes in social aggregates. The following categories are only idealized constructions for the general forms of development. Some types often have overlapping meanings given the limitation of the terminological linguistic possibilities of scientific language. So, these types are not meant to be sharply defined, but together, they rather indicate the space that the given inner dynamics occupies. There are three bigger groups of processes and states:

States and processes with prevailing homogeneous inner dynamics:
- coherence
- homeostasis
- recurrence
- simplification
- degeneration
- deceleration

States and processes with prevailing heterogeneous inner dynamics:
- expansion
- acceleration
- unification
- separation
- emergence of irregularities
- emergence of instabilities

States with prevailing neuterogeneous inner dynamics:
- primary chaos
- primary undifferentiatedness
- primary unordinariness
- harmonic coexistence

Let us briefly introduce several *ad hoc* examples that help us to imagine various instances within the field of anthropological inquiry. As apparent at the beginning of this chapter, coherence is a basic characteristic that enables us to distinguish man, culture, or society as systems with some sort of continuity in time. Without sufficient coherence, no entity could be distinguished and analyzed. But, when going into a lower, more specific level of analysis of processes with prevailing homogeneous inner dynamics, we can also find other realms where coherence occurs. Beginning with the basic forces maintaining any culture, coherence secures the maintenance of existing rules, norms, standards, customs, symbols, social scripts, ceremonies, and rituals in the cultural systems. The traditions in cultural systems exist because of homogeneous agency of coherence. Without any coherence, no traditions or other forms of repeated behaviors could be distinguished in cultures. Also, the use of a shared language that is understandable to most of members of an ethnic group is related to the agency of coherence in terms of the shared use of a coherent symbolic system of signs.

Homeostasis is very similar category to coherence, but it is much more related to the state of relative equilibrium in the inner environment of system. Homeostasis observed in human circulatory system is a typical example. In a similar vein, we may analyze the internal processes in towns and cities, which is an important issue within urban anthropology. Such processes may include the food supply for inhabitants, transport of people, or waste management. These processes of urban metabolism may or may not be in a relative equilibrium based on the operation of homogeneous inner dynamics with the character of homeostasis.

Recurrence frames the group of processes that share the feature of "something that is repeating". We may imagine various forms of recurrences, such as recurrences of very similar historical events in different historical periods. Historians sometimes say "history always repeats itself", and comparisons of historical events from different historical periods also support this thesis (e.g., Turchin, 2003). Also, religious practices such as rituals are repeated because of the homogeneous agency of recurrence.

In contrast, simplification means that some bigger system is decomposed into several lesser parts. Here, we can mention the dissolution of the Soviet Union. The unified republics of the former Union of Soviet Socialist Republics broke away between years 1989–1992, and became independent post-Soviet states.

This dissolution inside the USSR is an example of a process that can be categorized as simplification.

Degeneration has not only the character of splitting, but is much more related with the aging of subsystems or its functions. Degeneration may include dissociation, but the movement towards the decomposition of a system is key. However, such decomposition is not rapid, but gradual. The decimation of aboriginal Tasmanians by colonial pressures between 1804 and 1847 is an example of a gradual process leading to the end of this ethnic group. Thanks to the colonial power from another territory, this native ethnic group started to degenerate until it finally disappeared. The case of aboriginal Tasmanians is a typical example of the unequal relationships between a colonial power and an indigenous people. But it is also a good example of the opposing agencies of homogeneous and heterogeneous dynamics.

Deceleration has the dimension of velocity. In contrast to degeneration, deceleration does not necessarily imply moving towards a final collapse. It only means that something decreases its speed and moves slower. As an example, we can imagine the deceleration of economics during stages of stagnation. Such a stage shows the temporal deceleration of sectoral growth, but it will start to accelerate again when the stage of expansion returns. Kondratiev waves (Kondratiev, 1935) in economics show the dialectic between the opposing agencies of homogeneous and heterogeneous dynamical principles very well. Two opposing forces are always in the conflict, and the domination of homogeneous or heterogeneous dynamics is only temporal. After some period of the domination of homogeneous dynamics, heterogeneous dynamics begins to dominate again. So, economical development is suggested to be a constant process of dialectic clash, similarly to historical development as proposed by Yolles et al. (2008).

When turning our attention to processes with prevailing heterogeneous inner dynamics, in some cases, it is easy to merely switch the aforementioned examples. For example, it is simple to see the case of acceleration in the stage of the expansion of economics during Kondratiev waves as an example of prevailing heterogeneous inner dynamics. Furthermore, we can also return to the case of the decimation of aboriginal Tasmanians and analyze the example from the view of colonists. From this viewpoint, the decimation of the aboriginal ethnic group was forced by the heterogeneous inner dynamics underlying the behavior of colonists. Colonists were motivated to expand to another territory, and this is a typical example of expansion by the force of heterogeneous inner dynamics. The category of expansion generally implies a quantitative increase in size or an extension of existing system.

Undoubtedly, colonialism has much to do with intercultural processes. Acculturation is a process that has attracted the attention of anthropologists for many decades. During acculturation, one culture expands across its borders and changes another culture. This process may be accompanied by the transfer of ideas, technologies, customs, etc. It is apparent, then, that acculturation processes are potentiated by prevailing backwards heterogeneous inner dynamics. In contrast, the emergence of resistance groups within the population is a process of maintaining coherence. Members of resistance groups reject the acceptation of new cultural standards in attempt to preserve their culture of origin. Again, the dialectic between opposing agencies of homogeneous and heterogeneous dynamics is apparent.

The process of unification can be demonstrated on the example of emergence of the European Union. European states have started to share the market, some legislation, and in part, governance. These changes are understood as to be unification, and they are in contrast to the process of separation. We used the case of the dissolution of the Soviet Union as an example of simplification that is a process with prevailing homogeneous inner dynamics. But, when we switch the perspective, we may also detect the processes of the emergence of instabilities in the same case. The particular separatist movements inside the former states of USSR were potentiated by the prevailing heterogeneous inner dynamics, and they can be considered to be a case of the emergence of instabilities in systems finally leading to the process of separation. This example also shows the interrelation between two consequent processes in social aggregates. First, the instabilities that emerged in the systems, and consequently, some of the states of the former USSR started with the separatist movements.

Generally, many processes of any kind of change are considered to be processes with prevailing heterogeneous inner dynamics. Stages where the behavior of systems show prevailing heterogeneous inner dynamics are stages when systems may grow, evolve, and also differentiate themselves. However, differentiation itself is also a key principle that is suggested to be responsible for the emergence of social inequalities in social aggregates. Intergroup alterity especially is a case when one group has differentiated itself from another group. When one group gains more power, it usually starts to favor the ingroup and to differentiate the ingroup's image from the relevant outgroups. The emergence of social inequalities and stereotypes towards marginal groups is often present during this process. We do not want to go into more detail here, but on the general level, the differentiation between two social groups can be understood as a source for the emergence of alterity in the social system.

Here, we shift out attention to the key question of processes with prevailing neuterogeneous inner dynamics. As stated above, neuterogeneous inner dynamics maintains harmony, order, and equilibrium between the opposing agencies of homogeneous and heterogeneous dynamics. Neuterogeneous dynamics is neutral in terms of homogeneous and heterogeneous agencies, but it has the agency to stabilize both opposing agencies. We argue that instances where neuterogeneous inner dynamics would be prevailing are really very rare, and that some of them are rather hypothetical instances. For example, harmonic coexistence is considered to be a hypothetical instance. When social systems are still existing, it is highly unlikely that they would stop their differentiation for a longer period of time. Sometimes, we may distinguish that some social aggregates are temporarily in relative harmony in terms of the powers of social groups, the absence of intergroup conflicts, etc. But, this state is always temporal. Agencies of either homogeneous or heterogeneous dynamics start to influence the inner dynamics of a social system after the short flash of inner equilibrium. So, even though the state of harmonic coexistence is alluring for many social scientists, many decades of anthropological and sociological investigation throw us back into the rough reality of perpetual dialectic clash between agencies of homogeneous or heterogeneous dynamics.

Other cases are those instances when the order of a social system has still not been established. These instances are situations at the beginning of existence. In these situations, we can observe primary chaos, primary undifferentiatedness, or primary unordinariness. All three states are relatively similar and describe the initial states of existence. The term primary chaos highlights the chaotic behavior of possibilities or potentialities at the beginning, i.e, "when something is coming into being". Primary undifferentiatedness and primary unordinariness include the absence of order and difference. No kind of difference is present when things are at the initial state of primary undifferentiatedness. Similarly, no order can be found when things are at the state of primary unordinariness. All three of these states are unique and unrepeatable. They are states that can be considered as initial conditions in the field of chaos theory (Kiel and Elliot, 2004).

In the previous text, we briefly outlined the main forms of the life trajectories of man, cultures, and societies. Of course, our categories do not mean that just one type of process always underlies the processes observed in man, cultures, or societies. The ideal types are not mutually exclusive, but combinations and mixed types are rather suggested to occur. This fact complicates anthropological inquiry, but we should keep such hypothetical mixing in mind if we do not want to reduce such complex phenomena, i.e. cultures and social aggregates. Thus, it may be reasonable to expect the various combinations of these pure prototypical forms in highly complex nonlinear quantum systems, such as cultures, groups, and societies. These highly complex systems are attracted by strange attractors, and therefore, it is difficult to make strict definitions of the ideal types of their internal processes. The typology is thus rather indicative.

There are also some questions that are very difficult to answer at this moment. For example, the role of attractors in guiding life trajectories of cultures and social aggregates is not clear.

OPEN QUESTION FOR FUTURE RESEARCH 7
What function do strange attractors have in guiding the life trajectories of man, cultures, and societies?

This question transcends our current scientific knowledge; we believe, however, that we should not fear to posit such types of questions, since they can fruitfully stimulate future research, as well as future theory development.

Chapter 9
Death and Final Collapses
of Cultures and Societies

As we observe the existence of man and social units in time, we can also distinguish that neither man nor social aggregates remain permanently over time. Life as an equivalent of quantum coherence (Wendt, 2015) can be maintained only under specific conditions in both external and internal environment of a system. These conditions under which life is possible mean those conditions under which the system is stable enough to maintain its existence (as a coherent manifestation in time and space). The system dies when these conditions change over the frontier limits that are indispensable for the perseverance of the existence of the actualized potentiality. At this moment, the continuity of quantum coherence is broken, and the radical transformation of matter and energy often follows. After some time, each man dies and each social unit undergoes the radical transformation that can be called final collapse. There is no permanency that can be found in the lives of man and social aggregates. Man and social units represent two different levels of anthropological inquiry, and therefore, this chapter also will start discussing the case of death at the individual level, and only then we will shift to the case of the radical transformations of societies, groups, and cultures.

During life, the human body undergoes series of changes with episodes of destabilization of the inner environment of the body with impact on the whole system. This means that the configuration of the basic particles of the system is broken. As the collapse is approaching, the frequency of crises increases, and the range of changes in the configuration accumulates. This is true even in case of sudden death, e.g. a car accident or a heart attack. In this case, collapses of the system's elements happen in very short time interval, so they may not be easily recognized. Still, however, crises and partial ("small") collapses of elements or subsystems precede the "big", final collapse of the whole system.

According to many folk religious and spiritual beliefs, there is still something that survives this final collapse of the human body. Man is believed to be an aggregate of a material body and a nonmaterial self. While the material body is mortal, nonmaterial self ("soul") is suggested to be eternal, and thus survives the death of the body. What is fundamental to many religious and folk ideas about life after death is cyclicity. Cyclicity is one of the fundamental laws of nature often expressed in cultural symbolism. For example, the wreaths that we place on graves even today on All Souls' Day are symbols of eternal life. The image of the Phoenix, who after his death in a fire is born again, can be another nice example of nonlinear thoughts about life and death.

In folk ideas about death, earthbound life is then perceived as just a part of the "whole" life, as just one sequence of a longer process. Death is perceived as the final collapse for the material body, but a transformation for the eternal soul, which can remain in the realm of eternity or be born again within the body.

The western concept of soul is rather complicated. It is often, in the religious, in the philosophical, or in the psychological tradition, somehow connected to individuality. So, the eternal life of a soul indicates the eternal continuation of an individual with a particular identity. Subjective individual identity is given by the "I" sense generated by the subjective mind.

In many non-literate traditions, the notion of soul is not strictly bounded, there are also concepts of multilateral souls. During our stay among the Benuaq people of Kalimantan, where we conducted research on their rituals, we encountered special performances oriented to various souls. To put it simply, we can say that the Benuaqs distinguish a soul connected with the body, which stays in the "village of dead" that mirrors the world of the living. This soul needs to eat, drink, etc., and can feel joy or sorrow or other emotions in the same way that a living person does. It is the duty of living descendants to provide this soul with everything that a soul needs in the afterworld. It can also trouble the living people if it feels joyless. The second soul, connected to the head, is formless and resides in the realm of heaven. The Benuaq concept of soul fuses individual (emotional) soul with the formless "something" that outlives the body (Lorencova, 2008; for a detailed discussion, see also Venz, 2013, 2014).

All of these examples show man's attempts to deal with an idea of a nonempirical dimension. There are many notions and concepts, and it is not the task of this chapter to prove or to reject them. Rather, we aim to show how different conceptualizations of the world around us can shift the concept of the invisible realm. We also wish to show how concepts of quantum anthropology could be applied to this issue.

We can state that death and dying is the most controversial process in an individual's life. There are many interested groups and individuals who propose different suggestions, from the notion that death is ultimate to the notion it is just crossing over to other realms of (eternal) life. For materialists considering matter to be the fundamental element of reality, the death of the body is a final point of a life trajectory. Of course, the individual body with a particular identity no longer exists after death. However, this does not mean that the matter that constitutes a human body disappears. Rather, the basic particles which constitute the body are re-involved in the whole matter potentia. With new actualization (materialization), particles are rearranged into other forms and structures.

It is likely that just because of our limited senses; we often conceptualize man as a materially bounded body. According to this common concept, self is matter-dependent. This would mean that self ends with the visible surface of our body. However if we accept that human body has also quantum character (Wendt, 2015; Barad, 2007), as mentioned in the chapter on embodiment, it is not only matter that we are dealing with. We can see the human body as an actualization, a specific form spreading out of energy-information potential. Furthermore, as suggested by Barad (2007), it is presumable that the human body does not end at its skin, the surface being the object of our empirical experience. Most likely we may consider the human body to be a matter-energy-information complex.

Since the time when Moody (1975) introduced the concept of near-death (and out-of-body) experience to the western world, there have been many records and much research carried out about how individuals feel their self. Whatever people experienced during their physical collapse (cerebral death), they always experienced it as self-experience. Their stories often started with: "I left my body" or "I saw my body lying lifeless under me" (Kübler-Ross, 1992; Moody, 1975). People with near-death experiences speak about their self being formless with no limits of time or space, and, of course, with no limits of their body. Body is perceived just as a casing or vehicle. During near-death experiences, there is no direct connection with the body in the sense that "I" has no control of body movements nor does it feel pain. But cognition (even changed), thinking, and the feeling of emotions like sorrow, surprise, or all-embracing joyfulness was preserved during cerebral death.

According to the orchestrated objective reduction theory (e.g. Hameroff, 1998; Hameroff and Penrose, 1996, 2014; Sahu et al., 2013), the consciousness of man is understood in a quantum perspective, and it is supposed that it does not end with brain death (and possibly remains in a different realm). On the essential level, the consciousness of individuals is hypothesized to emerge from the so-called universal consciousness, which has existed for at least as long as matter (Hodgson, 1991). Hameroff and Penrose (1996, 2014) then postulate an often-criticized idea, that our experience of consciousness is the result of quantum gravity effects in microtubules in the brain. After the death of the brain, individual consciousness dissipates to the universe, but in the case of successful resuscitation (e.g. in the case of cerebral deaths), microtubules continue in their processing and quantum information returns into the microtubules. The experience of the universal consciousness is then perceived as a near-death experience.

What happens, however, if the collapse is really final? Hodgson (1991) argues that there is no straightforward individual survival after the death of a person. He understands person as an expression of some more universal underlying mind (universal consciousness). From this point of view, each person is considered as a unique node of connection (link) between this universal mind and the experienced reality. Thus, when a person dies, this unique structured link between the reality beyond the self (universal mind) and the reality beyond the experience (common objective world, matter) is destroyed. The unique structure of each link is what makes each person and each self unique. A person with its particular psychic characteristics (personality, feelings, abilities, interests, etc.), that made him/her different from others, did not exist prior to its actualization (conception) and will no longer exist after his/her death (Hodgson, 1991). The self is then limited in time, and this limitation is bounded by individual's life span. In contrast, individual consciousness in Hameroff's sense (Hameroff, 1998; Hameroff and Penrose, 1996, 2014) is hypothesized to exist before conception and will continue to exist after death.

This assumption is in the same vein of logic as the materialistic explanation of the afterlife existence of the material elements that form the body. As the decomposition of a material body is not a question of seconds, we argue that also the decomposition of an individual is not so quick. Of course, a body without a mind is just a body without free will, decision-making ability, etc., but it takes time until the matter is decomposed. Bones can remain in the grave even for thousands of years, and yet still contain components enabling us to reconstruct the "picture" of the individual. We hypothesize that our nonmaterial self is not immediately lost when returning back to the realm of potentiality; rather, it may gradually weaken its coherence. When the person dies of natural causes, the self starts to decompose often even before the final collapse, and the concept of self and world is shifted during the process of dying.

This gradual return of individual nonmaterial self back to the realm of potentiality is reflected in many religious thoughts and practices. Bardo of Tibetian Buddhism or Purgatory in Christianity could be examples of such "in-between" states. Also, the traditional notion of multiple souls reflects this conceptualization of gradual decoherence, as a series of rituals are conducted in connection with situation of releasing souls (Lorencova, 2008).

Hodgson (1991) asks, if a person survives death in a straightforward way, what would a person be? He argues that what survives is not the person as we know them at any particular moment of his/her life, but it is only the essence, which is not specific of the person. However, human experience with occurrences around the time of death is not so easy to handle, especially in anthropology, where we must deal with concepts of revenants or of meeting dead people in the altered state of (collective) consciousness. Something still remains that singularizes a particular person from the others and makes them a unique individual. Although there is no scientific evidence of the existence of "ghosts" (there is no possibility to measure them), reports about revenants are more frequent than it would be desired. Human experience throughout the history is full of modes how to cope with these encounters, and our language also carries different conceptualizations of soul, spirit and ghost.

Appearances of people who have died an unnatural death are experienced mostly in the places of their death (and not at the cemetery) – e.g. apparition in old jails, places of battle, murder sites, etc. A particular dead person appears repeatedly in the same form – the same clothes, similar movements, the same age, the same scene, etc. It seems that one configuration of the person's appearance gets stuck in space and time and repeats itself as a loop.

During shamanic rituals, it is very common that the shaman leaves to a "different" world, which mirrors our world, and they meet with people who live there. These people and all things have their "proper" form, so they look like they are from our world. The shaman can even meet with a particular individual and pass on a message from or to living descendants. In this case, we are not describing the materialization of the individual, but the experience of them in the nonempirical domain. However, in both cases, the concrete person can be identified. Unfortunately, nothing is yet known about this individual's consciousness or about their feeling of the self. It could only be supposed that there is no self-consciousness.

We speculate that information about personal unique structures stays in collective consciousness as a footprint in the sand. It is just in our everyday reality that we distinguish past and future and experience time as continuous flow from one point to another. In the nonempirical realm underlying our empirical (material) world, time and space are no longer limited. We suppose that in the nonempirical domain, all potential patterns remain, including the potentialities once actualized.

When we turn our attention to a higher analytical level, also societies, groups, and cultures sometimes meet the point when their existence ends, or a radical transformation occurs. From this standpoint, external anthropological observers cannot speak about the same group or culture. In the case when the existence of a social group ends, no direct continuity can be found with a future emerging social group, although the existence of the former social group may leave some heritage for subsequent forms of social life. The same can be said for cultures. Cultural evolution does not consist of separate periods of existence of particular cultural patterns. Continuity is always present, although this does not mean that we can speak about the same cultures.

Radical transformation in our understanding means that most of the basic elements of a particular culture have disappeared. After radical transformation, the former basic structures and elements are no longer present. This absence means that external anthropological observers cannot identify the culture as they could before the moment of radical transformation. It is apparent that it always depends on the analytical apparatus of researchers. In some cases, however, an agreement about the end or the radical transformation can be reached. This moment can be considered to be the final collapse of the culture.

How do the final collapses of cultures or groups come about? One of the authors of this book has explored this issue in his previous study (Trnka, 2015a). When a group approaches final collapse, the collapse announces itself in the form of crisis in the social aggregate. What is the relationship between a crisis and an impending collapse? In cultures or groups, each crisis can indicate an impending collapse of the entire system (Bárta, 2013). Thus, a crisis can be said to herald an impending collapse. It is an indicator of destabilization that already hints at a future radical transformation of the system. Crises are periods of destabilization in social systems. Commonly, periods of crisis alternate with periods of relative stability. This amplitude is characterized by continuous alternation of stable and unstable periods in cultures and sociopolitical orders. What is interesting is that as the moment of the collapse approaches, the frequency of individual crises increases, and the intervals between them become shorter (Bárta, 2013). Each crisis thus can be said to be a herald of the final collapse, such as the collapse of a given social system or even civilization.

Collapses are a part of the natural course of things, and we have noted many of them throughout the history of mankind. They are sudden and fundamental changes in the given system. At this moment, the system is transformed and fundamentally reconstructed. Simultaneously, though, it does not indicate the complete end of all existence, because with each collapse, the possibility for the emergence of something new is created (Trnka, 2015a). Nothing lasts forever, and the temporalization of complexity in its entirety through the temporalization of elements or subsystems is evident in the sociocultural meta-system. Crises and collapses are not unnatural phenomena, because the very functioning of a system is based on the mutual interdependence of extinction and reproduction (Luhmann, 1995). Thanks to this continuous decay, systems with a temporalized complexity are forced to continuously change their states.

What does a collapse actually look like in general? The collapses of societies or cultures cannot be observed, which presents anthropology with a serious methodological problem. Let us pose the question: at what moment exactly can we describe a society as being in a crisis? The fact that we label certain historical periods as being a crisis is definitely the result of our social construction. Social crises are usually not an objectively measurable reality, but depend on how the given situation is interpreted by the media and by influential people whose opinions form the public opinion of the members of a society. From this perspective, some social phenomena are really of an interpretative nature, and the opinions and attitudes towards them at that moment contribute to the social construction of the crisis. Therefore, the very act of observation can have a transforming effect on the observed reality, and so the nature of this reality may be heavily influenced by this social construction. To speak about objectivity or about an objective reality is thus not substantiated when it comes to social phenomena.

Fluctuation and change are typical for the dynamics of societies and cultures. The period of destabilization of such systems is often described by the term crisis in our everyday language. We can consider a society or a culture to be in crisis, a political system to be collapsing, etc. In reality, the state of crisis is a mere outcome of the accumulation of previous, less obvious changes in the system, which can be sometimes directly observable, but we do not give them a greater significance. Gradually, these small changes exceed a certain limit, and the system becomes destabilized, and at this moment chaos and the accumulation of crises begin to have a nonlinear character. This all hints at the impending radical transformation of the entire system – a collapse. In the course of the collapse, the changes may be relatively sudden, precipitous, and with a turbulent dynamics.

Most systems display an alternation of periods of stability with phases of instability, and in general, all systems try to return to a state of equilibrium in order to preserve their existence (Luhmann, 1995). Destabilization may occur thanks to both the inner environment of a system and to the external factors that stem from the environment of the system. Whether a system survives such a destabilization or crisis then depends on the degree of destabilization and the resilience (or resistance) of this system. In some cases, the system breaks down; it collapses.

As already mentioned above, in the case of various social groups and cultures, one cannot directly observe the course of the collapse. What is certain, however, is that this course is dynamic, and that it is impossible to predict its ensuing development. A collapse is a radical change in the development of the system, but this general characteristic is insufficient for a deeper analysis of this issue. What is the actual form of a collapse in general? What shape and course can a crisis trajectory take before it collapses? These are the questions that should be further explored in order to advance the theoretical analysis of crises and collapses, including their mutual relationship.

Trnka (2015a) discussed the possible dynamics of the radical transformations of cultures and groups in terms of hypothetical cycle, or spiral. A cycle is generally a description of a sequence of a chain of events that has the tendency to repeat itself. From a certain perspective, we can also understand the spiral as a description of a cyclical sequence of events; however, if we consider a spiral in the three-dimensional space, its shape hints at the factor of a time dimension. If we should consider the chains of individual moments of existence in time, then the typical movement of spirals with a time dimension is a helix. In general, the shape of a helix better characterizes the dynamics of collapse than a straight, one-way development, which very rarely occurs in the macroworld.

We argue that the basis of spiral movement stems again in a dialectic between two binary opposites, i.e. in opposing agencies of homogeneous and the heterogeneous inner dynamics (the basic characteristic of these dynamics was explained in the previ-

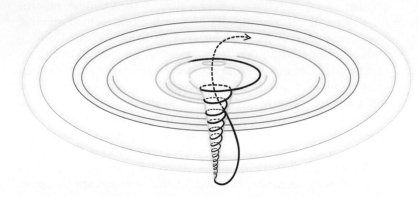

Figure 6. The spiral model of collapses in social and cultural systems (according to Trnka, 2015a)

ous chapter). If the homogeneous and the heterogeneous inner dynamics are in a relative equilibrium, movement along the trajectory is stabilized in an even helical shape orbiting around its central axis shaped in a straight line. If, on the other hand, the system reaches an unstable phase, the regular spiral movement is disrupted, and the spiral movement now has an either ascending or descending tendency. In this case, the individual threads of the helix either continuously grow or continuously shrink, creating the shape of a conical helix. The central axis can either be straight or however curved. For example, we can witness such types of movements in the macroworld with whirlpools, tornadoes, hurricanes, etc.

We believe that this parallel is inspiring for the concept of the course of the collapses of social aggregates and cultures. Bárta (2013) pointed out that the frequency of individual crises increases and the intervals between them decrease with the approach of the impending moment of final collapse. This type of development mirrors the shape of a funnel, or of a circular cone with a convex wall whose surface narrows up towards its peak. This idea has also inspired Trnka's (2015a) spiral model of collapses in social and cultural systems (Figure 6).

The spiral model of crisis leading to the final collapse is supported also by some mathematical models describing the behavior of collective systems. For example, Bhattacharya et al. (2009) provide such a mathematical model (Figure 7). In this case, the cone is an attractor for the convergent spiral trajectories coming from the external environment of the system. Such trajectories are constitutive for the system from the moment they begin to collect in the space and create a cone. This moment mirrors the initial conditions for the final collapse. These trajectories emerge from the uncertain chaotic possibilities and when coming into the cone, they acquire certain position. This model shows very well the importance of the sensitivity for the initial condition. The period when final collapse begins is thus of key importance for the determination of the further development of social unit that is approaching final collapse. After trajectories in the model enter the cone, they started to twist towards the narrowest part of the cone. Bhattacharya et al. (2009) point out that they are con-

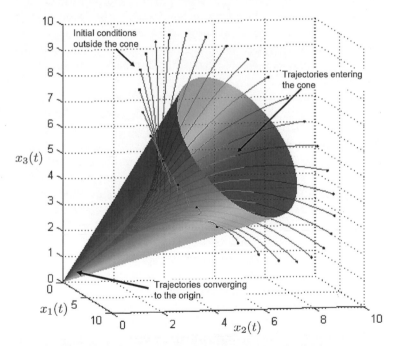

Figure 7. Bhattacharya's model of the dynamic behavior of collective systems (Source: Bhattacharya et al., 2009)

verging towards their origin, and when we look at their graph, the origin is just zero, i.e. nonexistence.

Bhattacharya's model indicates that the final collapse is attracted by a single point attractor. It is in contrast to the emergence of cultures and social aggregates that have been suggested to be attracted by some kind of strange attractors in Chapter 4. The final collapse is a process that ends existence. It is the move from existence to the zero state, i.e. to nonexistence.

Bhattacharya's graph is finite, when trajectories reach the zero point, they end; they have disappeared. On the other hand, however, Trnka's (2015a) spiral model of collapses (see Figure 6) also considers the possibility of returning to the realm of zero states, i.e. to the realm of potentiality. The moment of collapse is represented by the narrowest part of the conical helix, and after a specific entity or system decays, the existing manifestation of the energy-information field passes with the help of topological inversion back into the overall, wave-particle energy-information potential (see Trnka, 2015a, for more details). The given part of the energy-information field then again becomes a part of the realm of potentiality, i.e. the quantum potentiality field in terms of Puthoff's quantum sea of zero-point fluctuations in the vacuum (2002).

The consideration of returning to the realm of zero states enables us to accept the possible continuity between systems that have already died and systems that shall emerge in the future. The previously actualized part of the energy-information field becomes a part of the realm of potentiality again, so it is also possible that some of this constellation may be again manifested in the form of future actualizations. As we have mentioned above, when the existence of a social group ends, no direct continuity can be found with any future emerging social group. Also, the agency of a new group is different from that of the agency of the former group. We are, however, speaking about material bodies of group members here, and not about their individual consciousness. And this is the point. Even if material bodies die and the individual consciousness of group members return back to the realm of potentiality, similar patterns may emerge in the future both on the individual, as well as collective, level. This continuity between those systems that have already died and systems that will emerge in the future is indirect. Such type of continuity is specific, because it includes return to the realm of zero states, i.e. to the realm of nonexistence. This realm is not the realm of actuality, but it is the source of emerging patterns. And, as we have mentioned earlier in this book, the emergence of individuals or social groups depends on the type of strange attractor that is responsible for a given actualization. We can say that a strange attractor "selects" a part of the realm of potentiality that is proceeding to manifest itself as some kind of material or nonmaterial actualization in time and space.

The role of strange attractors is very important for sociocultural anthropology, because strange attractors predetermine agencies of individuals, and therefore, also the agency of any kind of social group. If we speak about agency, we should keep in mind that the strange attractor itself is an agency underlying the agency of any kind of social group that is already a manifestation of a part of the overall, wave-particle energy-information potential. It is an "agency beyond agency", and it is also a source of diversity and variability between people, national cultures, ethnic groups, subcultures, etc.

Another question is how the selectivity of strange attractors works? Why are emerging systems attracted only by some types of strange attractors? Is this process random, or not? Here, we are afraid that this problem extends beyond the possibilities of currently available scientific knowledge. Further development of this reasoning would be speculative at this moment, but it provides promising incentive for research in this area for future.

Chapter 10
Language, Collapse of Wave Function, and Deconstruction

In the eighties, Derrida's concept of deconstruction (1997 [1967]) influenced the writings of some social and cultural anthropologists. Textuality, textual reading, and the relationship between text and meaning represented one of the key concerns of postmodernism in this period. Deconstructive reading makes revealing hidden meanings in the text possible, and again underlines the relativity of anthropological methods.

A question that has been so far is what qualities does the process of deconstruction have? Here, we attempt to provide an interpretation inspired by the quantum anthropological thinking. It seems that the deconstructive reading of texts has a character similar to one phase of wave function collapse. How does a wave function collapse proceed? Before wave function collapses occur, the wave function spreads out over the entire space (Pusey et al., 2012). Each constituent of matter or energy does not have a clearly defined position in this phase. All things have the properties of a wave under the situation of non-collapsed wave function. At the moment that an external observer observes the wave, it peaks and the wave collapses in the sense that it actually has null values in all other places of the space where the given entity was not observed (Pusey et al., 2012). At the same moment, the observer starts to perceive the observed, e.g. the human body. The chain of wave function collapses ends at the moment when the observer stops their observations and turns his/her attention to another part of reality. After that, the wave function spreads out over the entire space again.

We argue that the process of deconstruction works in the same way. Meanings stay in the superposition state before the deconstructive reading of an anthropologist. In this phase, meanings of the text cannot be completely known. We may characterize this situation by the multiplicity of possible meanings. Before carrying out a deconstructive reading, the text may convey several possible meanings, and each of these meanings has a certain probability of coming into being. When the text is critically read, some of the possibilities are actualized, and an anthropologist pursues some of possible meanings of the text. It is due to reader's agency that only some of the possible meanings are appearing to his/her consciousness. After a deconstructive reading, the text returns back to the state before the reading, and the possible meanings remain in the superposition state again. Indeed, these fundamental characteristics of the process of deconstruction explain why textual and literary analysis is often declared to be irreducible and unstable. Each researcher may get different meanings from the text, and thus the subjectivity of a researcher plays a central role in the textual and literary analysis. The acquired meanings are, therefore, always relative and depending on the subject, i.e. the researcher in this case.

The idea that meanings stay in the superposition state before the act of reading interferes well with Ingarden's theory of reader experience (1973a, 1973b). It assumes that texts only represent incompletely determined states of affairs, and that "places of indeterminacy" are always present in texts (Bundgaard, 2013; Chrzanowska-Kluczewska, 2015). The concretization of text, or "gap-filling", always depends on a reader's action. It is apparent that Ingarden's conceptualization of the relationship between meanings and texts supports the quantum anthropological interpretation of meanings staying in the superposition state before the reading of a text, as is proposed above.

Derrida's (1997 [1967]) contribution highlighted the role of mutual relations between words, and pointed out that it is the network of these structures that makes language a language. Allow us to make several remarks on the nature of language here. Human language is suggested to be an informational system that has the character of a symbolic system (Patee, 2013), i.e. abstract system of signs. It consists of a relatively stable set of basic elements, signs/letters/words, and rules about their use, for example, codes or grammar. This does mean that signs have stable meanings over space, time, and contexts. Words are understood to be symbolic vehicles that acquire meaning in the process of communication or textual analysis. Human language is such a complex system that it enables us to express all varieties of thought, with the exception of some extraordinary states of consciousness like peak experiences. Peak experiences are experienced often in altered states of consciousness, and individuals have reported it is not possible to provide an exhaustive description of them when using a common language.

In contrast to thoughts, meaning is an emergent quality that is generated in the process of communication or textual analysis. Whereas thoughts are virtual and belong, therefore, to the realm of potentiality, their expression in a sentence is an actualization in time and space (Schäfer, 2008). A thought exists in the mind of a sending actor long before it is expressed in a form of sentence. When unexpressed, a thought is a part of a nonempirical reality, but when expressed in words, it is a part of the empirical world (Schäfer, 2008).

We argue that emergence of meaning in communication share some similarities with the probabilistic logic of quantum theory, more specifically with the theory of superposition. Many words have more than one fixed meaning. Linguists speak about denotations and connotations, or about explicit and literal meanings. During the speech act, the actual meaning of word emerges when a speaker conveys a message, e.g. speaks a sentence to a listener, or to more listeners. We argue that the emergence of meaning has a character of actualization in time and space. When words/signs are chained and sent to a listener in a form of a code, the actual meaning emerges with respect to a given situation or context. We suggest that the multiplicity of meanings in some words is given by the superposition of meanings that a given word may be linked with. Before the actual message is generated, the word may convey several meanings, and each of these meanings has a certain probability to be actualized. When a message is generated, one of the word's meaning is actualized (depending on the context that the word appears in), whereas other meanings are not actualized. From this perspective, the denotative meaning is the meaning that has the highest probability to be realized in comparison to connotative meanings in a given culture.

In a similar vein, Wendt (2015) suggested that the ground state of a concept is represented as a superposition of potential meanings. Concepts shared in a given culture are understood as vectors within their wave functions. These vectors are in superposition, being entangled quantum mechanically. They have different weights, mirroring typicality of meaning, i.e. how typical the meaning of a given concept is. These weights are related to the probabilities of how likely will the concept collapse into one actual meaning. The speech act is suggested to be what elicits the collapse of a concept's wave function from potential meanings into one actual meaning. The speech act is thus believed to be analogical to the moment of measurement in quantum mechanics. The collapse of concept begins with the intention and decision of a speaker to communicate some of the meanings to a listener. However, the actual meaning is always produced contextually, i.e. it depends on the context of event and listener. From this view, memory structures and agencies of both speaker and listener are intra-acting in the same way as measurement devices in quantum experiments intra-act with microparticles. The introduction of a new concept in communication has the potential to significantly change the follow-up development of a communication episode. Similarly, the change of material or virtual context of communication may have significant influences on meanings that are actualized. There is also some empirical evidence available supporting the notion that quantum entanglement and interference are present in actual language use (Aerts, 2010).

We shall continue in this line of thinking and develop this idea further. We argue that the speech act is not the only instance when the collapse of concept's wave function from potential meanings into actual meaning may occur. At the beginning of this chapter, we focused our attention to the act of reading texts. The intra-action between the agency of a reader and the agency of author by the meaning of the text is present, and therefore, we state that aside from speaker/listener intra-action, reader/text intra-action should also be taken into account. Although the text is not a living entity, material configuration is also suggested to be responsible for the generation of meanings (Barad, 2007). From this view, the text can be regarded as an intra-acting counterpart of a reader, and therefore, the collapse of concept's wave function is suggested to possibly occur by the intra-acting between reader and text. Meanings stay in the superposition state before reading, and collapse into actual meanings when a reader intends to and begins to read. So here, agencies of both the reader and the author of the text are intra-acting in the same way as agencies of speaker and listener during a speech act. And again, the actual meaning is always produced contextually, not only by the circumstances accompanying the act of reading, but also by the intended meanings and structural unity of a text. Thus, pursuing the meaning of a text during textual and literary analysis is related to the concept's wave function and the act of reading itself.

Furthermore, we argue that quantum entanglement exists also in the realm of the mutual relationship of signs and words. Derrida (1997 [1967]) suggested that signs exist only in relation to each other. The meaning of one sign exists only in relation to another sign or sings. Words may obtain meanings only because of contrast between signs. This relationship is similar to the relationship that is supposed to exist between microparticles in quantum mechanics. Microparticles do not exist as separate entities, but are always entangled. The quantum state of each particle cannot be described independently of other particles. So, we argue that the emergence of meaning is possible only because of the quantum entanglement of signs in a particular language (for the hypothetical qualities of such quantum entanglement between signs see, e.g., Merrell, 2009).

Let us turn our attention to a general relationship between language and thought. The sharing of language by the members of a given cultural group is well-evidenced, but the nature of such cultural sharing is questionable. For example, Wendt (2006) built a maybe too excessively sharp dichotomy between the externalist and internalist view of cultural sharing. He distinguished between the internalist's "thought precedes language" position and the externalist's "language precedes thought" position. Individualistic sharing supposes that thoughts are assumed to reside first inside in the individual's mind and only then may become common knowledge. In contrast, the holist or externalist view supposes that the meanings of our thoughts are intrinsically social, constituted by thoughts in other people's minds, i.e. "language precedes thought". Yet actually, we do not think that either the first, neither the second relationship should be omitted in the integral concept of quantum anthropology.

When viewing them in a dynamic manner, both instances are justified and may occur in quantum social systems. The quantum anthropological perspective does not reject that various cultural elements may be transferred between individuals, as well as between groups and representatives of institutions. Such types of transfer may be included in the process of learning, for example. If the source of transferred elements is intrinsically cultural, based on actually shared traditions, values, or standards, this is the case of externalistic sharing, and here, "language precedes thought". On the other hand, when a social actor actively changes or modifies some of the existing cultural standards and transfers it via communication, it is an example of individualistic sharing, and then "thought precedes language". In that case, the social actor plays an active role in changing the existing cultural standards. To refuse one of these two distinct instances would be reductionistic. If we would strictly refuse the role of externalistic sharing, it may imply that no recognized cultural standards exist or may be distinguished. On the other hand, if we strictly refuse internalistic sharing, social actors would be suggested to play only a passive role in the culture/individual relationship, and also, the instance of inter-individual learning may then be problematic to justify. For these reasons, both instances are very important for a complex understanding of the ongoing process of the differentiation of social and cultural systems. Moreover, when the relationship between language and thought would be supposed to be unidirectional, such an idea would not meet the complementarity principle, which is one of the basic pillars of quantum logic (Bohr, 1928). Thus, we suggest that the relationship between language and thought is bidirectional.

Language plays a key role in Foucauldian discourse analysis (Foucault, 1972). Society is being shaped by languages of specific discourses that reflect the existing power relationships. In this theory, discourse is understood to be the totality of language used in a given field of social or intellectual practice. The social world is supposed to be expressed through language and practices. We argue that specific forms of patterning may be observed here, because various discourses differ in the structure and language use. Discourses are perpetually differentiating toward each other, and the term inter-discursivity describes this alterity. We expect that inter-discursivity has also the character of quantum entanglement, similar to the quantum entanglement existing between signs. Similarly to microparticles, discourses also do not exist as separate entities, but are always entangled.

(121)

The entanglement between discourses is, however, approachable only on the higher analytical level than the entanglement between signs, which is rather settled within a specific cultural environment.

Barad (2007) has contributed to the quantum understanding of discursive processes by highlighting the importance of the material configuration of the world. Language is no longer seen as an exclusive foundation of discourses. The transparency of language is questioned, and its mediating function is rejected. Fixation on words in anthropological analysis is suggested to be reductionistic when trying to fully understand reality in its entire complexity. Instead, the material configuration of the world and the differentiating patterns of mattering are believed to be important for the performance and boundaries of meanings. The primary semantic units are not words, but material-discursive practices (Barad, 2007). It implies that not only social actors, but also matter itself has its own agency that may reconfigure the meaning. The world is seen as an open process of mattering, through which mattering itself acquires form and provides a fundamental background for discursivity and inter-discursivity.

The ontological inseparability of matter and action is known as the entanglement of intra-acting agencies. The process of intra-action is understood as a process by which the boundaries and properties of the components of phenomena become determinate (Barad, 2007). In the case of human culture, concepts become meaningful in the process of intra-action between material configuration and human action. Phenomena are understood to be differential patterns of mattering, produced through complex sets of intra-acting agencies of multiple material-discursive practices. The reality is seen to be perpetually constructed in the dynamic process of intra-activity and materialization. It is because of this ongoing flow of agency that phenomena come to matter. Therefore, the continuity in the life trajectories of discourses exists. But, the world is not static, and vice versa, entanglements and relationalities are changing in time and space and are considered to be perpetually changing topologies of the world.

This kind of reasoning about language, meanings, and inter-discursivity opens a new, exciting field for further discussion. The quantum understanding of meanings enables an exploration that may have serious implications for other related issues, for example, for the way the occurrence of symbols in everyday life could be theoretically conceptualized. Therefore, we utilize this connecting link and turn our attention to myth, symbols, and the agency of collective memory in the following chapter.

Chapter 11
Myth and Entanglement

When approaching the phenomenon of myth and its mutual entanglement with a social system, the concept of mythopoeic system should be defined first. The mythopoeic system is a society's entire body of sacred cosmological symbolism, including the symbolism found in myth, ritual, mobiliary and architectural arts, drama, performance, sacred landscape and games (Laughlin and Throop, 2001). The mythopoeic system is one of possible explanations for the expressions of reality in our everyday lives, e.g. life events. It mirrors the cosmology and the symbolic representation that formed a particular cultural system. Each culture (and the global culture as well) has its mythopoeia, and this mythopoeia consists of various ratios between culturally shared scientific beliefs, the symbolism of traditional mythopoeic systems (often interconnected with spiritual beliefs), myths diffused by global media, etc.

At the beginning, we would like to focus on the underlying principles on which mythopoeic systems are created. We argue, as stated in previous chapters, that the emergence of any system must be based on some kind of underlying zero states. This statement is applicable to the mythopoeic system as well. According to Merrell (2009), a sign is supposed to emerge out of the "emptiness", "nothingness", or zero state. This process of emergence presupposes the necessity of interactions between our brain and the quantum sea (Puthoff, 2002). The question which has still not been satisfactorily answered is whether this interaction is direct or not. Despite some suggestions of direct interaction (Laughlin and Throop, 2001; Popp, 1998), we must also take into account the alternative possibility of an indirect, mediated relationship.

Also according to Merrell (2009), the emergence of the sign from emptiness is not direct, rather, we can recognize a mesophase between the absolute emptiness and the actualization in time and space. The empty set is the phase when a sign enters into the range of concrete possibilities. As mentioned in the chapter about collective unconscious, the empty set is something that happens to be empty, the "noticed absence" of something that was or could have been or might possibly be there partially or wholly to fill the unoccupied space (Merrell, 2009). It is probable that archetypes, which we understand as tendencies or quantum patterns underlying representations, occur in this mesophase known as empty set. The predicted mesophase lies between the realm of initial potentiality, i.e. quantum vacuum energies or overall wave-particle energy-information potential (Trnka, 2015a), and the manifestation of archetypes in the world, i.e. in the form of images or symbols.

Archetypes are basic constituents of collective unconscious, they are invisible and nonempirical. This means that the elements of myths are originally timeless and non-local, stored in the collective unconscious, from where they are actualized and possibly expressed in myths. They appear as sacred symbols transformed into the collective consciousness and individuals' minds. Collective unconscious is thus considered to be a primary source for mythology and symbolism. In this sense, mythology serves as a vocabulary useful when experiencing the transcendental dimension of reality. For example, during altered states of consciousness or near-death experiences, the appearance of a white shining figure is often reported. Even though the form or shape of this appearance is very similar, people from different cultures and with different experiences use various formulations or images to describe it. In western culture grown up on the Christian tradition, the shining white figure is often connected with Jesus, God or an angel, which is different from, for example, the Indian or Muslim tradition. There are also reports of small children who describe this figure as a kindly woman, angel-woman, or Mary (see, e.g., Kübler-Ross, 1992; Moody, 1975). We can suppose that to reproduce and give meaning to their extraordinary experience, people try to use the closest concept or archetypal image they are able to retrieve. We can also understand archetypes as early patterns of experience that structure our experience throughout our life, thus in this sense, it is deeply foundational and influential (Knox, 2003).

Jung (1959, 1983) understands his archetypes as inheritable tendencies to form such representations of a motif – representations that can vary a great deal in detail without losing their basic pattern. Jung's archetype is the underlying structure (pattern) forming the definite mythological images or motifs, not the motif or image itself. Jung's idea of archetypes is derived from the notion of elementary ideas, which are products of the physiological mechanisms of human brain, so that the mental acts of all people from different cultures are the same.

Also, structural anthropologist Lévi-Strauss (1963) was influenced with this neuroscientific assumption when analyzing the universal structure of myths. He supposed that similarities have their origin in the underlying biological structures of our cognition, and thus, in this context, he pointed to the universal structure of the human mind. According to him, the grammar-like rules that govern the production of myth exist within the brains of people, while the expressions of myth are just particular transformations. Continuing in this influential biogenetic approach, Laughlin, McManus, and d'Aquili (1990) postulated that neurognostic structures underlie all true mythology. According to them, mythical stories:

> "... are the expression of both (1) the fundamental neurognostic structure of the human brain, and (2) the content appropriate to the varying environmental and cultural existencies characteristic of a particular society. The neurognostic structure of myth comprises what we might call the universal cosmology upon which virtually all traditional cosmologies are grounded and are transformations."
> (Laughlin and Throop, 2001, p. 720)

The universal cosmology is then mediated by living cells being self-organized during neurogenesis, reiterating an ancient system of knowing with each generation. Nevertheless, according to new findings in quantum science, the human brain operates not only on classic mechanisms, but also on quantum processes (e.g. Hameroff, 1998). Neural processes are no longer considered to be only locally determined transmissions, but new findings in quantum neuroscience enable us to turn our attention to "something" that transcends individual brains and the simple computational level.

If we were to change the perspective, we can move from the biogenetic structuralistic understanding of archetypes as the essential structures of the human brain (or psyche) back to the Platonic concept of forms, which could be understood as the essential structure of reality (or the universe). Platonic forms are non-local and atemporal essences of various objects. They are unchanging underlying patterns, without which objects (things) would not be the kind of themselves. These forms are the essential basis of reality, which even means that they are superordinate to matter. Despite of this, or perhaps therefore, Platonic forms are non-physical, nonempirical, and non-visible, and they do not have ownership of individuals' minds

The concept of Platonic forms is just the shift of the focus from the man-centered perspective to the universe-centered perspective, and from man as a system to man as a subsystem of a higher system. According to systemic theory (Luhmann, 1995), each subsystem is formed within a system, so the evolution starts with the system which is in a certain way transformed into the to-be-created subsystems (Grandpierre, 1997). We can say that the structure of this subsystem is made by the creator system. In this holistic sense, it could be stated that the human mind and the universe are ordered according to the same archetypal structures.

Despite of his attempt to find universal structure, Lévi-Strauss (1963) noticed that we can find contradictory motives and states in myth. We can claim that, in myths, anything can happen. It seems that myth lacks any logic, continuum or rules; it behaves almost chaotically. Especially the non-canonical myths of native non-literate cultures are influenced by continuous chains of alterations. Studying, for example, the native traditional mythologies of Kalimantan, we have found a variety of alterations in stories and a variety of their meanings for specific people. For instance, the authors still remember their own first experience with the, native Dayak concepts of everyday and sacred experiences which could give of the impression of something contradictory, illogical, and confusing. However, it is necessary to realize that just considering multiple ontologies can be a good basis for the experience of alterity (Alberti et al., 2011).

We can state that mythopoiea is a dynamic process, which reflects the trends and changes in the social, cultural, and natural environment. Thus, it is questionable if attempts to find universal structure could be fruitful. It is also questionable what kind of structure could be found in reality. It is probable that we would obtain not a universal structure, but a structure of our own thinking bonded by our own experience, culture, official knowledge, personal concepts, beliefs, etc.

In this sense, the way to solve the confusion of equivocation could be inspired by the perspectival anthropology of Viveiros de Castro (2004), who stressed that our attempts in anthropological investigation should be focused on these equivocations themselves. These equivocations emerge when two conceptual languages comes into contact. Equivocations are not what impede the relations, but that which finds and impels them, they are the differences in perspective. In this sense, multiple realities exist if we accept the notion that an object's existence is more than a point of view onto reality, but a reality in itself. We can find these differences between cultures or species, but also between individuals. From the point of view of quantum anthropology, those who are the observed and those who are the observer (object-subject relationship, or self and other relationship) play a crucial role in the appeared alterity between actualizations.

Meanings embraced in myths may be actualized in a similar way as the meanings of words in a sentence (as recognized in previous chapter). The constitutive particles of myths, which Lévi-Strauss (1963) calls mythemes, representing irreducible, unchanging elements, can acquire meaning only in relation to another mytheme or mythemes. Mythemes cannot be described independently of other mythemes because they are entangled in a quantum sense – this means one element has to be interrelated with others. In this quantum perspective, the elements of myth share some similarities with quantum probabilistic logic. We suggest that there is a multiplicity of meanings of single mythical elements given by the superposition of meanings that they may be linked with. In this sense, actualization of meaning may be interpreted as wave function collapse. Before the actual meaning of myth arises, the mythical elements may convey several meanings, and each of these meanings has a certain probability to come into being. The actualized meaning depends on the context of the observer and his agency.

The mythopoeic systems are often strongly entangled with the social systems where they are embedded. The symbolic images used in myths arise from the particular environment being a frame for everyday human experience. For example, animals such as bears, tigers, wolves, or hyenas, or other carnivorous predators, are often used as symbols of some evil or danger. Which type of animal would act in the particular myth depends on the local geographical distribution of the species. The same can be applied to plants and other creations of nature, the landscape (such as a forest, a desert, mountains, the sea, etc.), but also to the particular products of sociocultural order (such as social institutions, social roles, etc.).

This entanglement may result in that a big part of the members of these cultures share a similar mythology. We can say that most people accept and participate in accordance with the world view they inherit from their culture. This participation results in real life experience that is, in turn, interpreted in terms of the mythopoeic system serving as the confirmation of the people's system of knowledge (Laughlin and Throop, 2001).

It is difficult to estimate the extent to which myth shapes the scripts for the everyday lives of the members of a culture, but the entanglement between a mythopoeic system and individual minds might be quite strong, as all children are exposed to myths and fairy tales in the course of their early development. These stories may have a crucial significance for the cognitive development of prototypical social scripts, concept formation, and also the formation of identity. Thus, the agency of myth starts to influence the minds of people from a very early age.

In this perspective, we can see myth as collectively shared (and thus also accepted) evidence of experience with some special instances that are embedded into collective memory. The experience of the hero in myths, no matter if they are a warrior, holy man, or laundress, resonates with the individual's experience on the ontological level. This experience can bring us into contact with the essential human dimension and the basic conditions of our lives (e.g. mortality and vulnerability, identity, relations, needs, etc.). The experience embraced in myth is often perceived as our internal experience. This feeling of consonance does not come automatically, but rather if we make (or have personally come to know) such an experience, it means if we are receptive. It means that not all members of the sociocultural group share the same relation to mythical themes. Rather, the process of "acceptance" is, to a certain extent, selective on the conscious level given by the course of a life trajectory. This is valid, especially, in the case of vertically and horizontally extended experience (see Chapter 2).

The power of the myths is grounded in their meaning-creation potential. In this sense, experience in myth serves as the context to give meaning to our experiences. In myth, however, the border between character, notion, and the time-space position is not clear. For example, in ancient Egypt, *maat* was the term for truth, order, justice, harmony, and stability, but *Maat* was also a goddess with her own cult and genealogy. So, we are dealing with the principle maintaining and underlying Egyptian society, and simultaneously with the anthropomorphous goddess of this principle. This logic is not only connected with ancient or "savage" ways of thinking, as we can see in the case of Barthes' chapter *Soap-powders and Detergents* (1993), where he analyzed the myth of products which became used in (not only French) everyday life. As he says, products based on chlorine and ammonia are the representatives of a kind of absolute fire or blind warrior, while powders, on the contrary, are selective, they just push or drive dirt through the texture of the object, so their function is keeping the public order, not making war. The principle of "negative" evil, violent and dangerous, which we need to be on guard against, and the principle of the "positive" maintenance of order are connected with the specific objects (products) of the individual brands.

The meanings encoded in ancient and traditional, sacred stories, as well as non-spiritual, medially diffused stories, shape peoples' orientation in their everyday lives. The mythopoeia informs the lived experience of people and gives it sense in their lives. The entanglement between experience and myth is apparent. In mythical stories, experience is registered in such a way that the listener lives and conceptualizes the experience vicariously through internally generated feelings, thoughts, and images – through the ostensibly imagined adventures of the hero or sacred being. Moreover, the didactic quality of myth makes it possible for people to share the same body of core symbols and the sacred context in which the symbols are applied (Laughlin and Throop, 2001).

As mentioned above, listening to myths and fairy tales is a child's primary symbolic experience. This experience is indirect, and it proceeds without actual physical contact with the world. While listening, children identify themselves with the characters, experience the story and events, and learn how to solve prototypical situations. Even though they do not understand the whole depth of wisdom embraced in the story, they absorb it on the unconscious level. This helps for the development of prototypical social scripts and scenarios in their minds. Heroes in fairy tales provide "role models" for children, which enable them to identify with socially accepted social roles and emotional behavior.

It is one of the characteristic features of myths that have the unceasing capability to purvey subsequent insights and understandings. As the individual or the whole group grows and gathers experiences, new meanings of the myths actualize. These actualizations serve for new interpretations and conceptualizations of meaning. Meaning in myth is not objectively given, even though some "official" meaning is expected in the sociocultural group. For individuals, however, mythology is a continual source of meanings that appear. In this sense, it can be seen as a sea of potentiality.

Even though the human language is such a complex system that it enables us to express all varieties of thoughts, experiences behind the ordinary order can be expressed only to a limited extent. Mythical language can interconnect everyday experience with the experience that transcends it, e.g. with the extraordinary states of consciousness (trance, near-death experiences, dreaming, meditation, etc.). It is the special quality of the myth that the wholeness of reality is recorded so that those states that are ordinarily contradictory states are connected together.

The language of myth is mostly metaphorical and symbolic. Metaphors or symbolic expressions are not the intention, however. Rather, metaphors have to be used due to the limitation of our language. And thus, for people without near-death experiences, e.g. the motif of the "loving, all-embracing light", it is just a metaphor, but for people with near-death or out-of-body experiences, it means a shift to the level of the universal understanding on the totally existential experience. As not everyone has this experience, the symbol of the "loving, all-embracing light", depicted as radiance, could be understood as just an image or metaphor.

(131)

The relation between symbols and the invisible transcendental reality is reversible. This means it is not just that symbols emerge from transcendental reality, but that they also act as a way of connecting with the transcendental realm. The use of symbols or primordial images connects and guides an individual's or group's mind to the invisible domain of reality. Every religious tradition has its set of symbols, archetypal in the core, that enables its adherents to reach the transcendental sphere. Numbers, signs, masks, or archaic formulae are believed to be able to change the structure of everyday empirical reality, so the identity (what makes it "it") or quality of the objects can be changed. It could be, for example, the symbolic sign of the holy cross before the first slicing of bread, which extends man-made bread to the extended realm of the sacred sphere, or the Christian tradition of writing C+M+B signs supplemented with year (e.g. 20 C+M+B 16) over the doorway of a house, church, or other buildings on January 6, the Epiphany, which also serves as a connection to the sacred sphere (to obtain a blessing).

In any case, individuals are not only passive actors in relation to mythopoeic systems. They can actively modify and change the existing mythology. Upon occasion, it can lead to alterations in interpretations, which in turn can change aspects of the cosmology, and the ritual-mythopoeic reflections of that cosmology found in a particular culture (Laughlin and Throop, 2001). The experience of myth goes hand in hand with action – action that is repeated. In this sense, myth is entangled with ritual, drama, performance, or other human action throughout the process of its coming alive. The resurrection or creation of a mythology accompanies the resurrection or creation of a new tradition, which brings new actions, relations, values, meanings, explanations, etc.

During our anthropological field research of the Czech neo-Slavic communities, we have observed a mythical resurrection which enabled adherents to create and understand their identity roots, ritual activities, values, and group relations. The most important neo-Slavic rituals (Figure 8) take place during the transient phases of the year, i.e. solstices and equinoxes. The core of these rituals lies in the experience, which constitutes the basis for the formation of sense in ritual participants. This experience is extended both vertically and horizontally. In the case of

Figure 8. A practicing neo-Slavic shaman during the resurrection of a Slavic ritual during the autumnal equinox, St. Donat, Czech Republic, 2012 (Photo: Radek Trnka)

the horizontal extension of experience, we have to stress that the archaic ritual practices of Slavs have not been preserved until the present in Czech culture and written historical records. Thus, the neo-Slavic shamans have to be inspired by other Slavic countries where some fragments of myths and practices remain and are still practiced. The recent Czech neo-Slavic shamans resurrect the ancient Slavic symbols and concepts, but their own ritual practices are rather experimental. Shamans play an active role in the construction of practices that are mythology-related. In the course of rituals, they actively explain meanings of the speech, actions, and symbols which are present. These explanations reconstruct the probable design of rituals and mythology based on indicative fragments from historical records of various Slavic ethnic groups, but the construction is strongly shaped by the shamans' subjective influences. Explanations of meanings which

(133)

are declaimed during rituals are the fundamentals of the new emerging "myths of origin".

This effort is understood by adherents of the neo-Slavic cult as ritual and myth resuscitation, but in reality, it is rather a ritual- and myth-making process. Myth has the ability to mediate and give higher meaning and signification to the lives and experiences of the members of the social group. In this way, myths of origin help to objectivize and legalize the emerging subsystem of the sociocultural system. Myths and rituals also have the power to make the sacred from the profane.

Myths and mythical sacred symbols also have the power to create and maintain the sense of collective origin, and support the continuity of the social, ethnic, national, or religious group. Thus, a national cultures' mythopoeia always has a historical continuity with the mythopoeic system that shaped the consciousness of individuals for years, but it is also a product of the creative imagination of the members of a particular social system.

A cultures' mythopoeia is an informational spectrum based on both the individual and collective experience. Once created, the myths and symbols circulate among group members, and on the level of sharing, they have the potential to arouse emotions, which reciprocally make the myths and symbols even more sacred or special (Turner and Stets, 2005). In the course of time, the circulation and sharing of symbols becomes the particularized cultural capital of the group that comes through the words, special knowledge, speech patterns, objects, memories, experiences, and other things that are shared only by the members of the group. Once the group is symbolized, the invocation of the symbols alone will arouse emotional energy. It is the strange quality of symbols that they are able to connect people without the need of being co-present. Symbols can arouse the energy as long as individuals are able to recount past collective effervescence in memories (Collins, 2004; Turner and Stets, 2005). This is the case whatever the symbol is, be it a holy cross or a national flag.

On the other hand, collective emotions also have the power to generate new myths and symbols, as can be seen in the current migration crisis in Europe. In the contemporary era of the information and communication technology revolution with global media such as the internet, it is not necessary for people to create a group localized in time and place. Even though they are physically "alone", they still experience emotional arousal being shared on the collective level of "online". With the increased mobility and flow of information, there are also social systems of local cultures entangled with the mythopoeia of global culture through the virtual "online connection".

Chapter 12
Ritual, Observer Effect, and Collective Consciousness

Ritual occurs on the border of the empirical and nonempirical domain. It enables people to touch the world beyond and to connect both domains into one all-embracing reality. We can understand ritual as a special kind of human behavior oriented on transcending common natural laws and sociocultural order. From this point of view, ritual is a kind of practice which affects appearances and is able to transform them. While ritual is often perceived to be in opposition to everyday reality, in fact, ritual enables the extension of this everyday reality to a broader realm of possibilities, as we will see throughout this chapter.

"In a ritual, the world as lived and the world as imagined, fused under the agency of a single set of symbolic forms, turn out to be the same world" (Geertz, 1973, p. 112). What has been considered to be impossible is becoming possible because of the human ability to act upon and change the world. Berger and Luckmann (1966) argued that our world originates in our thoughts and actions. Changing our thoughts and action is undoubtedly the core of ritual practices. The lived and the imagined are experienced together as one reality during ritual. Things that "could be" are experienced as "they are". And subsequently, ritual can also cause a significant shift in values, social status, but also in physical health or quality of matter. We can consider the ritual to be a gateway from one alterity to another.

Everyday human reality is mostly empirical – this means that everything comes to us via our sensory perception. Kant (2006 [1798]) understood objects perceived by our (external or inner) senses to be appearances. The cognition of the object in appearance is then called experience.

"Therefore appearance is that representation through which an object of the sense is given (an object of perception, that is of empirical intuition), but experience or empirical cognition is that representation through which the object as such at the same time is thought. – Therefore experience is the activity (of the power of imagination) through which appearances are brought under the concept of one object of experience, and experiences are made by employing observations (internal perceptions) and through reflecting (reflectirt) about how to unify them under one concept."
(Kant, 2006, p. 31, footnote 24)

Entities which appear are experienced and manifested in a such way that they lie in the realm of culturally determined experience and worldview – in concepts. According to Kirby (2011), concepts are ideality, while things are materiality. The human mind interacts with concepts, and therefore, its memory structure is sensitive to them. There are neuronal networks in our brains that are sensitive to potentiality waves. The collapse of a potentiality wave leads to a new empirical structure. Potentiality waves trigger brain states, expressing in this way the concepts in our minds (Schäfer, 2008). Aerts (2010) argued that the nature of quantum entity is conceptual; it interacts with the measuring apparatus or with the material entity. Quantum entities are signs exchanged between measuring apparatuses, or more generally, between entities made of ordinary matter.

During the process of cognition, we interact with potentiality waves and choose one of the possibilities of how things could be. We can say that our everyday life lies (mostly automatically) on the reduction and elimination of inconvenient possibilities of how things could be. What possibility we choose depends on our limited receptors, the context of appearance and cognition, on previous experience, knowledge, actual mood, expectations, intentions, or priming. There are, of course, many other factors which could be more or less important in particular situations.

Reality as we see it (as it appears to us) when using our limited receptors is divided in accordance with the fundamental wave-particle duality – duality between the localized, visible, measurable, empirically observable reality (particles) and the non-local, invisible, nonmeasurable, and nonempirical reality (wave functions). In this context, concepts such as material and formal, physical and spiritual, or empirical and nonempirical are used (Schäfer, 2008). Entities and their manifestations emerge from the nonempirical domain, where non-observed, unselected possibilities remain hidden and wait for their potential future actualizations. This nonempirical domain is inseparable from the empirical domain, despite that in everyday life, it appears to be separated by a non-permeable border. We must emphasize here that the border of the empirical and nonempirical domain is affected by culture, which also affects most of our cognitive processes and experiences. It is obvious that every culture also produces behavior which enables overcoming this border. Such behavior may be, for example, magic practices, the private or ritual use of psychoactive substances, religious, or other collective ritual or ritual-like behavior (see e.g. Lorencova, 2010/2011).

Therefore, rituals function as operators connecting the minds of people with the realm of potentiality. In the practice of ritual, the observer effect is purposely utilized, which is very different from scientific practices, for instance, where the observer (researchers) unsuccessfully attempts to eliminate the observer effect. Entities which appear in ritual are experienced in the realm of so-called "extended potentialities". Actions and thoughts are affected during ritual, which has a strong impact on the perception and experience of reality, and vice versa.

Ritual behavior used to be distinguished from everyday activities on the basis of framing (here, the framing of rituals denotes the settings for rituals, not the perceptual framing introduced in Chapter 3). This framing needs special dress, place, time, activities, speech, or, at least, a special state of mind. Each of these components of ritual leads the participants to change their cognitive processes and experiences as much as possible. The special dress and masks or rhythmic music can serve similarly to the use of psychedelic substances.

Ritual framing is full of symbolism. In this sense, we can stress that symbols play a key role in ritual. If participants connect themselves with the nonempirical sphere where everyday cognition and logic are not useful, there are no appropriate thoughts and words in their minds and vocabulary, normally connected with their everyday life. Based on the flashes of experience with the nonempirical domain, symbols emerge and are maintained. During collective rituals, people transmit collective messages to ourselves, which are encoded in ritual symbols, the meaning of which is familiar to the members of a particular group. While the prescribed form of ritual actions serves as a road to the nonempirical domain, symbols serve as a map during the ritual.

To affect the observer effect and to elicit the creation of the field of collective consciousness, actions that change the states of mind of, at least, the charismatic persons (the shaman, the ritual specialist), are embraced during ritual. This can include mental work, meditation, physical deprivation, use of psychedelic substances, trance etc. In the course of ritual, the specialist (shaman) connects at first with the realm of extended possibilities through his charismatic action, and then he/she helps the other participants of the ritual to (more or less) reach this realm, too. The connection established this way spreads gradually to the other participants of the ritual, so that they share experience, emotions, incentives, and cognitions, being entangled with each other and also with something that goes beyond them.

Ritual action particularly accentuates beliefs, intentions, moods and emotions expressed in movements, symbols, and speech. Movements, symbols, speech, dress, time, and the other framing of ritual have a strong impact on mood, cognition, experience, and worldview. Moreover, collective ritual practices often contain synchronized behavior that leads to synchronized arousal, which runs into the flux of collective experience. Synchronized repetitive physical action enables cognition and the mind to be extended to the sacred sphere – to the realm of potentialities.

Shared experience creates the whole group's concepts about the perceived entities. During a ritual, two basic modes of synchronization emerge: synchronization that occurs within the participants, and synchronization between the participants (d'Aquili et al., 1979). In the course of a ritual, the internal biological rhythms of the participants become synchronized with the external rhythms produced by the ritual performance. The entire system of the individual and the collective system are under the entangled influence so that they merge into one organism (Rappaport, 1999). In this sense, we can speak of a collective body. Wendt (2006) went even further and proposed the concept of a superorganism allowing non-local communication among their members.

Other researchers have found that there is strong synchronization in arousal measured as heart rate (Konvalinka et al.,

2011). This finding was not related only to the performers' states, but the synchronization was observed also between heart rates of the performers and the spectators. Moreover, the synchronization is suggested not to be found only in the heart rates, but the whole organism is hypothesized to be interconnected and attempts to reach an internal synchronization.

We can also speculate that some kind of synchronization can be expected even between brain activities. At the subtle level of connectivity, the brains of individuals experience a strong field of collective consciousness supported by the neuronal processes of their separate nervous systems, which fall into a "simpatice" or resonance. This would be equivalent to a kind of quantum entanglement between activities in individual brains, and can be considered to be an example of the binding between individual consciousness (Combs and Krippner, 2008). The existence of synchronization on the brain level can be demonstrated on the research of the experience of emotions (Singer and Lamm, 2009) and the research of synchronization between heart and brain activity (McCraty, 2002).

As proven by the research of Konvalinka et al. (2011), once the collective body is created, non-local communication has been established. The heart rate synchronization studied in the fire-walking ritual was not related to the synchronization of physical activity, since participants and spectators often performed different kinds of movements. This has lead them to the conclusion that the synchronization of physiological markers shared among the participants of ritual was not caused by the exchange of matter or energy, but only by the exchange of information. This exchange of information is supposed to proceed on the unconscious level. We argue that the participants of a ritual may share information generated in the field of collective consciousness through the process of quantum entanglement.

We understand the field of collective consciousness during the course of a ritual as a shared feeling of "being together" in a single unified field of experience (e.g. Midgley, 2006; Ziman, 2006). We can call this togetherness "communitas" in the sense of Turner (1969, 1982). Communitas is the experience of the "blend" of sacredness and lowliness, homogeneity and comradeship, often described as a "moment in and out of time". A shining mutual understanding emerges on the existential level and

(140)

brings something "magical", subjectively perceived as a feeling of endless power.

Communitas is experienced in the realm of liminality, which Turner (1990) understands as fructile chaos, a resource of new possibilities and new forms and structures. It could be applied on liminality that "everything is possible", and we can understand liminality as the realm of potentiality in terms of the quantum anthropology presented here. Communitas is then a deep entanglement of individuals and the realm of potentiality. It can be envisioned as the communion of non-local brains within a networked mind (Moore, 2015). We can speak about ritual consciousness as an altered state of consciousness that transpires beyond the boundaries of the known.

Grandpierre (1997) stated that consciousness develops through the phenomenon of "emotional infection" because emotions have the nature of being shared by others, of extending the landscapes, and of entering into other field of consciousness. Emotions thus has an epidemic character, as they can be amplified into collective impulses or mass psychosis. Emotional energy increases with collective effervescence, particularly if it is accompanied with the symbolization of group relations through (sacred) symbols (Collins, 2004). With this emotional energy wave, a merging of the individual consciousnesses into one single common consciousness is enabled. Entanglement in ritual is not only the state of communitas in general, but also the observations made by the networked participants of a ritual (Moore, 2015).

During e.g. fire-walking rituals, participants walk for several seconds across a carpet of coal with a surface temperature around 500–700 °C without any harm. Some of performers walk more than once or dance in the fire, some of them hold somebody or something (ritual objects) on their shoulders.

Fire-walking rituals are special kinds of rituals. Many rituals are closely connected with religious or cosmological beliefs and are not transmittable. Fire-walking rituals are successfully practiced in western societies without their original cultural and religious context, and they still "work". Also, the motivations to conduct these rituals are different in western societies, ranging from group problem-solving or team-building to the individual acquisition of self-confidence or personal and spiritual development.

(141)

Some of these fire walkers would cross the carpet of glowing coal even outside the frame of ritual, however, most of them would not. It is obvious that many of the participants would roast their feet before they undergo the fire-walking ritual. Once involved in the ritual, they changed their states of mind so that it is possible for them to cross the glowing coal without any harm. Ritual participants are supported by ritual action, shared arousal, and they unconsciously interfere with field of collective consciousness. The border between empirical reality (how things are) and nonempirical reality (how they could be) crumbles during the performance of ritual, and other potentialities emerge and actualize.

According to quantum theory, elementary units of reality are no longer constituted only physically, but also by their wave functions. This means they are no longer identical with themselves, because wave functions are constantly becoming entangled with other wave functions (Wendt, 2006). The transfer of information based on quantum entanglement is strengthened by the energy of shared emotions, changing the perceived quality of matter. The mental act of an observer, i.e. the participant of a ritual, changes the physical phenomenon that appears only "in" and "through" them. According to shared common way of thinking in everyday life, and often confirmed by everyday experience, embers can burn – but during the ritual, the way of thinking changes and influences the appearance of a newly observed reality. Thus, people who normally would burn if they step on the embers are able to do so without any harm.

Wendt (2015) argues that human subjects are quantum systems and elementary units of social reality. Our wave functions themselves, then, would correspond to our unconscious, which is all of the background knowledge that we are not aware of when we are conscious. Since collective wave functions are instantiated in separate brains, their collapses are mediated by individual bodies and minds that remain a locus of control in the process.

Continuing with the example of the fire-walking ritual, we must remark that there are also people who get burned during ritual, as well as people who can safely walk on embers without any participation in the ritual. We suggest that both groups of people believe deeply in natural laws. The first group of them is confident that according to the laws of nature, it is impossible to walk across the carpet of embers; the second group is confident that it is possible to walk across it thanks to the laws of nature, so both groups use different kinds of physical explanations. Despite of the fact that the method used influences the appearance of the observed reality, it is always the observer who selects what will be observed. Persons deeply confident that there is harm or that there is no harm in fire-walking observe what they have selected according to their beliefs and concepts. Any of these possibilities can be actualized in their consciousness, and the observer effect may be hypothesized to be responsible for the safe (or non-safe) contact of the skin with the glowing coal.

Let us now turn our attention to the production of difference and alterity through ritual. Collective wave functions are not conscious, since consciousness emerges only in their collapse. But they structure action, enable collective memory and engage also in computation. The way in which collective intentions unfold therefore depends on how individuals express them. The consciousness of those intentions only emerges with the action (Wendt, 2006). Ritual action and intention are inseparable phenomena, just like the spheres of individual and collective. The consciousness of the "difference" is produced in relation to the whole, and this "difference" is a probability wave.

Schäfer (2008) understands probability waves to be empty. According to him, they carry no matter or energy, only the information on numerical relations. Information is understood as numerical relations, while potentialities are still mathematical forms. These forms are virtual states, or, patterns of information with the potential to manifest themselves in the empirical world. They are structures of quantum states and they exist independently of matter. If we want to change the matter, we must change the structure first. We have seen that ritual treats the matter right in this way. Ritual actions and intentions are focused on the change of structure, while matter serves as a source. For example, during fire-walking, the sole of the foot becomes resistant to burning, in the Christian mass, the Eucharist emerges from the piece of bread, in healing rituals, the disrupted matter of a certain organ is believed to be restored, etc.

During rituals where ritual specialists (shamans) walk in sacred landscapes to speak with ancestors and spirits, the structure of the everyday material world changes so it becomes unlimited by time and space. In this "differently" structured world, the ritual specialist can move without everyday limitations, and can meet things of past or future. Moreover, this structurally changed space-less and time-less alterity is entangled with the space we normally experience. During such rituals, participants of the ritual can see the movements and behaviors of the ritual specialist, which are very similar to the behavior of people with virtual reality glasses in a game arena. The material body of a ritual specialist is located here, but his/her experience of alterity comes from the realm of nonempirical reality.

Ritual is effective in the sense that it affects information underlying forms of potentialities. We can understand information as a function of the observer (von Foerster, 1988 [1973]), but also as the "difference which makes the difference" (Bateson, 1972) or "alterity which makes the alterity" (Alberti et al., 2011; Paleček and Risjord, 2012; Viveiros de Castro, 2004). Since it is not possible to separate the observer and observed, the difference/alterity lies in the observation itself. The concept of difference is so fitting that Umpleby (2007) believes it is preferable to speak in terms matter, energy, and difference. Difference/alterity is the basis of our cognition and of the concepts created in our mind. The maintenance of borders between these concepts is a crucial condition of our everyday order. Without these concepts and their borders, the world would be a chaotic place, where human beings would be lost.

Ritual represents a safe method to overcome the chaos that arises with the fall of borders. Our conscious mind works with actualizations. Actualizations cannot be in a direct contradiction, since our minds work with the difference. We are not able to believe in "A" and "non-A" at the same time. If a person believes, for example, that they can walk on glowing coals without any harm and simultaneously believes they cannot, it is very probable they will be perceived to be crazy in the eyes of other people. Reality should be the first or the second in a particular moment. If a person would hypothetically believe in both, a "difference" must still remain, because "A" and "not-A" cannot exist together at the same time or in the same location. The difference or alterity is often discovered in social circumstances. However, ritual uses a special framing to evoke the alterity and to extend beyond the borders of everyday experience. During this extended experience or alterity, what appears to be "A" is possible to experience as "non-A", too. We can say that both possibilities exist, but in parallel realities. Here, we must accept that parallel realities are an output of the observer effect.

As apparent throughout this chapter, human reality emerges from the observation and from practice. Human beings are not just passive observers; they are active, aware, and conscious. Consciousness is a constitutive feature of our life (Wendt, 2015). According to Wendt (2006), consciousness emerges in the collapse of our wave functions. This process happens continually as we interact with the environment, providing a basis for our experience of a "stream" of consciousness. Thus, ritual enables the extension of consciousness, and provides a meaningful connection between empirical and nonempirical reality.

Chapter 13
Conclusions and Future Directions

This book presents new insights and urges for the further development of anthropological theory. The core of quantum anthropology introduced here consists of the redefinitions of current anthropological concepts in the light of the new findings of quantum mechanics. We are aware that the reformulated issues presented in particular chapters are merely starting points for follow-up discussions rather than finite theoretical suggestions. But, as mentioned in the Introduction of this book, quantum anthropology is a relatively new perspective, and because of this, we have to accept that the conceptualization of the main fundamentals of the quantum anthropological perspective is still at its beginning.

Perhaps it could seem to be too early to speak of any basic principles of quantum anthropology at this moment. However, what else can be offered to the readers of this book as concluding remarks then to briefly summarize the main ideas that have emerged throughout the chapters. Therefore, we will briefly formulate the basic theoretical shifts below. The reader may find the more detailed conceptualizations of these ideas in the given chapters.

If we start with the main concerns of anthropological inquiry, we consider man, cultures, and social aggregates to be the actualizations of potentiality in time and space. All existing material, as well as nonmaterial, phenomena are derived from the fundamental substrate of the realm of potentiality. The realm of potentiality is understood as an overall, wave-particle energy-information potential (Trnka, 2015a) that includes an all-pervasive substrate for all possible actualizations in time and space. It is the source of the entirety of being and existence. Physically, the overall energy-information potential may be explained, for example, by the idea of the quantum sea (Puthoff, 2002), i.e. zero-point fluctuations consisting of the continuous creation and annihilation of microparticles in the vacuum.

Before any existence starts, zero-point fluctuations in the vacuum are suggested to be random and chaotic. We argue that some kind of quantum patterning starts to operate when an entity is coming into being. This patterning is hypothesized to be connected with the agency of attractors, the hypothetical states that have been previously developed in the field of mathematical modeling and chaos theory. We extend the function of attractors also to the moment of emergence. We argue that quantum patterning is attracted by the agency of some kind of attractor when an entity is coming into being in the initial phase of existence. It is called "agency beyond agency", because attractors operate without the agency of human actions or the agency of human products in the world. We consider the agency of attractors to be a deeper agentic level that operates out of human actions or the actions of human products.

Whereas previous efforts in the field of quantum consciousness have been mostly focused on individual psyche and the human mind, we have tried to go further and provide a quantum look on various collective phenomena, i.e. cultures, social groups, and collective consciousness. As mentioned throughout the book, all phenomena that man can identify are only appearances that come to man's perceptual capabilities. From this perspective, we also interpret the quantum nature of cultures and social groups. Such collective phenomena appear to us as if they have some kind of coherence in time and space. Despite that this coherence may be only a product of our minds, most ordinary people share this appearance and are able to reach satisfactory agreement in the identification of a specific person, culture, or social group. Here, we intentionally omit the assumption that every moment of reality is an absolutely new, disconnected quantum event, i.e. the flesh of existence (Malin, 2012). We do not refuse this assumption and believe that it can be fruitfully utilized in the field of quantum logic. In this book, however, we aim to provide a reformulation of the science of man. And this science, anthropology, accepts man's position in the world as is. In other words, anthropology accepts man with all of their limitations, including the way man is able to perceive and understand reality.

From this position, also accepting the limitations given by the observer effect, we also derived the following quantum conceptualizations of man, cultures, and social groups.

As apparent from the whole book, we consider quantum coherence to be the basic condition for the identification of man, cultures, or groups in time and space (see also Wendt, 2015). These phenomena are coherent enough to be identified by most people with satisfactory agreement. Also, the conceptualizations of man, cultures, or social groups accept the hypothesis of quantum coherence, which appears to our streams of consciousness in the form of chained frames. If we start at the individual level, man is understood to be an embodiment of a part of the overall energy-information potential (Russell, 2013; Trnka, 2015a). When a part of the overall energy-information potential is actualized, the external observer is able to identify a specific anatomical form e.g. the concrete human body in the time-space moment. Back to the moment of emergence, the human body, as well as the mind, is also related with the agencies of attractors that enable the quantum patterning responsible for the appearances of identifiable, coherent forms.

In contrast, cultures, groups, and societies do not have their own material bodies, which could be observed directly. Yet they still show certain forms of coherence in delimited time segments. Generally, we understand culture and society as an entangled quantum complex. We speak about the "sociocultural meta-system" or the "sociocultural reality", not about two simply separable phenomena. In other words, culture and society interact in the perpetual process of entangled mutual construction. This highly complex quantum meta-system can be only artificially deconstructed for the purpose of easier anthropological analysis. Through this deconstruction, social aggregate may be understood as a nonlinear, highly complex quantum system composed of the temporary interrelationships between its elements, i.e. individuals and groups. We argue that the interactions within such a system occur similarly to the perpetual interactions of quantum microparticles. Social bonds are perpetually changing in the sense of the ongoing reconfiguration of their structure in social systems. Everything in a social system is relative and in the process of permanent change in time and space. The behavior of a social system is not only the simple sum of interactions between individuals and groups, but there are also emerging actions that cannot be derived from the individual actions of social actors. Quantum anthropology understands individual human beings as the basic elements of a social system. And, it is the very interaction of individual agencies that is responsible for social dynamics, i.e. the perpetual creation, maintenance, or untangling of social bonds.

Some patterns of quantum accumulation create a quantum coherence that appears to us in the forms that can be called ethnic group, subculture, community, or family. But the behaviors of such quantum systems are also productive. Human minds produce various thoughts, incentives, and emotions. Human bodies produce various actions. We can observe that man acts in the world and changes matter through various practices. The results of such types of actions appear as material products. The activity of the human body itself is also productive, i.e. it is a behavioral manifestation of man in the world.

Culture belongs to one of most complex products of human minds and bodies. We understand culture as an informational spectrum created and shared by some of the members of a given social system. For better analytical purposes, we can deconstruct culture to include various cultural elements, e.g. beliefs, assumptions, attitudes, preferences, values, standards, interpretations, behavioral rules, norms, social scripts, prototypical actions, customs, habits, practices, ceremonies, and rituals. But, at the same time, we should also keep in mind the mutual entanglement of these elements. Cultural elements are not separate phenomena, but they are deeply interconnected.

Let us turn our attention to a more speculative issue, to the issue of collective consciousness. We suggest that collective consciousness is also a product of human minds and human bodies. There is a high number of different definitions and explanations of collective consciousness (see the chapter on collective consciousness – Chapter 7), but most of them share some general assumptions. Collective consciousness is hypothesized to be a kind of a field that emerges based on the processes of quantum binding, e.g. quantum entanglement. It is the extension of individual consciousness into a higher, collective level. During such quantum binding, the field of individual consciousness transcends the borders of the organism and interferes with the consciousness of another person or persons. Thus, some kind of connectivity between individual minds is supposed. These processes are difficult to imagine, but anthropologists often encounter them, at least in the case of rituals and other collective events.

The quantum coherence of man, cultures, and social groups does not ensure the absolute stability of these systems over time. External factors or the interaction of elements and subsystems inside the system often lead to decoherence, i.e. to the destabilization of the whole system. Such destabilizations are related to the agency of some kind of underlying dynamics. In the chapter about life trajectories (Chapter 8), three general forms of dynamics were proposed. Following the Hegelian dialectic, the conceptualization of homogeneous, heterogeneous, and neutrogeneous inner dynamics has been introduced (Trnka, 2015b). These three general forms of inner dynamics are suggested to potentiate and affect the functioning of systems in specific directions. They are not considered to be causal factors, but rather the inner characteristics of various developments and transitional states during the course of the life trajectories of nonlinear quantum systems. Homogeneous inner dynamics is generally characterized by an invariance and a tendency to return things to their original state of order, i.e. to the very beginning of their existence. Heterogeneous dynamics is, in contrast, a source of alterity, differentiation, diversity, and multiplicity. Heterogeneous inner dynamics stimulates change and the creation of various things; it stimulates production. And finally and thirdly, neuterogeneous inner dynamics regulate the opposing forces of homogeneous and heterogeneous dynamics. It serves to protect the existence and the stability of a system.

Despite the agency of neuterogeneous inner dynamics, the absolute harmony between homogeneous and heterogeneous dynamics can only be very rarely observed in sociocultural reality, and if it is observed, it always lasts only temporarily. The overgrow of homogeneous or heterogeneous inner dynamics may cause the destabilization of a system. If one or the other dynamics prevails too much, the system is destabilized and has the tendency to collapse. In such cases, it depends on resilience of the system, i.e. the effectiveness of safety mechanisms if the destabilization will lead to the final collapse or not.

Neither man, nor cultures, nor groups exist eternally. If the destabilization causes an overrun of conditions that are indispensable for the preservation of quantum coherence, the continuity of quantum coherence is broken, and the radical transformation of matter and energy often follows. We call this moment final collapse. Particular embodiment, i.e. a human body, is terminated at this moment. Similarly, when the existence of social group ends, no "direct" continuity can be found with the emerging social groups in future. The existence of the former social group often leaves a heritage for subsequent social forms, but such continuity can be rather considered to have the character of, for example, collective memory. However, collective memory is not able to ensure a "direct" continuity between the antecedent and the following social group. The final collapse in the sense of the radical transformation of a social system means that the newly emerged form of social life is not the same system as the antecedent social group, ethnic group, or community.

We have provided a very brief outline of the fundamentals of the quantum understanding of man, cultures, and social groups. There are many questions that arise. For example, it is not clear what effects the extension of individual consciousness into a collective level for the subjectivity of an individual may have? During rituals, mass panic, collective hysteria, or collective trance states, the fields of individual consciousness interfere and are extended because of specific kind of quantum entanglement. But what happens with the subjectivity of an individual in these situations?

Wendt (2015) defined subjectivity in terms of cognition, experience, and will. Will is suggested to be the "mental causation" of human action in the world. Cognition and experience are supposed to be passive and reactive, because they reflect rather than create reality, while will is understood to be active and purposeful. Will is considered to be responsible for causal powers, like the ability to cause physical movement (Wendt, 2015). However, if will is responsible for the activity and the productivity of human body, what happens to subjectivity in states when an individual's consciousness is extended into collective consciousness? Is it possible to expect that individual's will lose its autonomy when the individual's consciousness is entangled within the field of collective consciousness? And generally, how can the subjectivity, will, and human ability to act during the extension of individual consciousness into collective consciousness be changed?

Furthermore, another related problem is that the field of collective consciousness often arises based on the interference between individuals' emotional experiences. Wendt (2015) considered emotional experience to have only a passive role in man's subjectivity, but if we consider the case of the emergence of collective emotions, one can question this assumption. Despite of the fact that collective emotions are not suggested to be created consciously, by volitional effort, the roles of an individuals' emotional experience cannot be considered to be passive. We argue that without the interference of individuals' emotions, no field that we call collective consciousness is meaningful. This area is very rarely empirically investigated, and therefore, we may ask what is the causal role of individuals' emotional experiences for the emergence of collective consciousness?

Not so far from this question is the issue of the experience of alterity during altered states of consciousness, e.g. trance states during rituals, dreaming during sleep, meditation, clinical death, or intoxication by psychoactive drugs. Perceptual abilities are changed in these states in comparison to normal states of consciousness, but what about subjective experience? The experience of alterity is present without any doubt, but how can such a form of alterity be understood? One opinion may be that experience in altered states of consciousness is artificially built based on hallucinations or altered percepts. But, for example, dreaming is a natural process that does not need to be triggered by any psychoactive substance or by the volitional performance of special practices like hypnosis or meditation. So, we can also posit the idea that a normal state of consciousness is only the product of historical discursive practices and the discursively-formed knowledge of the world-consciousness relationship. If we deconstruct the classic idea about the normality and the givenness of "normal" states of consciousness, we can consider a more relativistic view of experience of alterity during altered states of consciousness.

In Carter's (2014) framework (see the chapter on empirical and nonempirical reality – Chapter 2), we may see such a relativistic view of subjectivity and individual experience. Subjective experience may not be evaluated according to any discursive notion about normality, but it can be simply seen as to have multiple layers and the potential to be possibly extended into different experiential realms. The multiplicity of experiential planes can be understood in a pluralistic manner. We may simply accept the fact that various people can experience alternative realities, and that the possibility of shifting between realities exists (Alberti et al., 2011) – both horizontally, as a perspectival shift between the internal logic of two different cultures, and vertically, as the ex tension of consciousness into higher-dimensional branes (Carter, 2014). Such types of thinking may contribute to a higher pluralization of our worlds and support a symmetrical understanding of various cultures as well as alternative states of consciousness. From this perspectival view, altered states of consciousness may not be seen as something pathological, but rather as an experience of alterity and as participation in alternative realities. We suggest that it is this very perspectival anthropology (e.g., Alberti et al., 2011; Paleček and Risjord, 2012; Viveiros de Castro, 2004) that may benefit from considering both the horizontal and vertical shifts of perspectives in the future investigation of man.

The main building blocks of the theory of quantum anthropology introduced in this book are based on the interplay between the realms of potentiality and actuality. Simply put, things that can be observed empirically are things that constitute the realm of actuality. However, what is more problematic is the key question of how to understand randomness versus patterning when an entity is emerging from the realm of potentiality? We will explain this problem in more detail below.

Undoubtedly, alterity exists in the world and is expressed via the enormous variability of human bodies, minds, and ontologies (Alberti et al., 2011; Paleček and Risjord, 2012; Viveiros de Castro, 2004). This variability is not infinite, however. Across time and space, it is possible to identify some occurrences of similar patterns appearing in the realm of actuality. By this, we mean the similar personalities of two people, similar cultural elements, similar ontologies, similar social fields, or similar human practices across different cultures. We do not argue that absolute sameness can be found, and we rather speak about "relatively similar" and not absolutely the same patterns. But, on the other hand, there is an overall potentiality that we call the overall, wave-particle energy-information potential (Trnka, 2015a), and this overall potential is supposed to be composed of the random, continuous creation and annihilation of virtual states (Puthoff, 2002). The random creation of possibilities is hypothesized to be infinite in the vacuum. There are fleeting electromagnetic waves and pairs of microparticles that perpetually come into being and back again into nonexistence. The overall, wave-particle energy-information potential covers random flashes of microparticles without any continuity. The absolute randomness in the vacuum collides, however, with the expression of potentiality in the empirical, observable reality. If alterity in the world would mirror the absolute randomness in the vacuum, then the occurrences of similar patterns should not be expected.

It is important to suggest that the absence of the continuity and permanency of randomness in the vacuum are different qualities than can be found in the chaotic behavior of entities in our everyday reality, i.e. in the realm of actuality. In already actualized systems, the spontaneous order usually emerges after a period of chaotic behavior. So, if an already existing system displays chaotic behavior, after some time, the chaotic behavior of the system's particles will start to either cause the final collapse or shall change their behaviors and begin to form various clusters. Such emerging clusters represent the origin of a new, emerging order in the system and also a modification of random alterity. It is a source of self-organization in the system, indeed. The situation is far different, however, than that in the case of the random creation and annihilation of microparticles in the vacuum. Here, the permanency of randomness can be found. We may therefore posit the key question of how is the emergence of similar patterns from the random, overall, wave-particle energy-information potential possible?

On the general level of analysis, the occurrence of similar patterns appearing in the realm of actuality means that two or more actualizations have been attracted by a similar kind of attractor. But indeed, this assumption implies that the variance in creation, and therefore also in alterity, is not infinite. If the variance in creation would be hypothesized to be infinite, then all actualizations in the realm of actuality should be unique and different from each other. No similarities would be present in the hypothetical case of absolutely infinite variance in creation. But, as mentioned above, it is not the case of entities and systems that

(154)

can be empirically observed in the realm of actuality. Thus, we may accept that the variance in creation is finite.

However, what is responsible for this finiteness of creation, for limited alterity, or for the occurrence of similar attractors in the time flux? We offer several alternative answers to this question to provoke follow-up discussions on this issue.

First, one possibility is that the emergence of similar patterns could be explained by the probabilistic logic itself. Some constellations of initial conditions can be considered to be more probable than others. If we realize an enormous number of actualizations that have been observed during history of scientific observation, one may consider the possibility that some similar patterns might occur, simply, because of a very high number of repetitions. In one thousand people, it is likely that we find two or more people with very similar personalities or physical appearance. And similarly, in one thousand cultures, it is likely that we find two or more very similar cultural elements, or ontologies. From this point of view, the emergence of similar patterns could be explained by the impossibility to ceaselessly create new and absolutely unique patterns. It can be hypothesized that as the number of actualizations increases during time, the probability of the emergence of two similar patterns increases, as well.

Second, it is also possible that the position in the sequence of creation is more important than the number of repetitions. Russell (2013) pointed out that at the moment when an individual actualizes one of the potential possibilities of his/her life, all other potential possibilities collapse into one specific, embodied act in the continuous action or "coming into being" in space and time. Our past actions and decisions limit our infinite potential for future actions, and some trajectories of our next development are highly probable, whereas others are highly improbable. Therefore, if we imagine the analogy with the development of historical events, one may expect that the actualized historical events influence the probability of occurrence of future events. We suggest the hypothetical idea of sequentiality that determines the emergence of future forms. Simply put, the position in a sequence of creation may determine the appearance of future actualizations.

Third, the agentic influences of conditions in which new emergences arise may be considered to be another source of finiteness.

Both physical conditions, i.e. matter, and sociocultural conditions may be taken into account. Matter enables some kinds of creation, but not others. In the same vein, for example, the macrocultural environment enables emergences of some kinds of microcultures, but not of others. The conditions surrounding new, arising existence represent the initial enablement for creation. This enablement may be the explanation for the limited alterity and finite variability of creation.

Fourth and finally, it is also possible to expect that some kind of proto-information exists out of the realms of potentiality and actuality. The overall, wave-particle energy-information potential (Trnka, 2015a) is considered to be the basic substrate for all actualizations in time and space. This quantum potentiality field includes pre-existing information for the future actualizations in the form of the qualities of microparticles in the vacuum. Yet these microparticles are continuously created and annihilated. No stable aggregations, patterns, or proto-forms can be found in the vacuum. Thus, the overall, wave-particle energy-information potential (Trnka, 2015a) may be considered to be formless in principle. Here, we realize that some actualizations are influenced by patterns that could be called Platonic forms, archetypes, or forms settled in the mental plane of Carter (2014). We may only speculate that some set of proto-forms exists out of both the realms of potentiality and of actuality. As already mentioned in the chapter on collective unconscious (Chapter 7), the hypothetical idea about some kind of intermediate state may be taken into account. We may consider the possibility that these hypothetical intermediate states are proto-information serving for the actualizations in the realm of actuality. This idea is analogical to Merrell's (2009) idea of the empty set. The empty set means a hypothetical mesophase between absolute emptiness and the specific actualization in time and space. In the case of quantum anthropology, absolute emptiness can be understood as continuous creation and annihilation in the overall, wave-particle energy-information potential (Trnka, 2015a), whereas the empty set or proto-information may be considered to be some type of prefiguring pattern responsible for the specific actualizations.

As seen on these speculative contemplations, more research is definitely needed to shift our current understanding of the realm of potentiality forward. Also, many other issues presented in this book share the same requirement. Researchers in the field of quantum mechanics have shown us that our reality is of a different nature than we believed before. Every scientific period in human history is based on the certain belief in some kind of paradigm. We are aware that also the quantum view of reality is only another step in the chain of scientific discoveries. For now, however, the scientific belief in the quantum nature of reality demands the actual redefinitions of key concepts in the social sciences and the humanities. This book is meant to provide new inspiration for future researchers in this field, as well as to contribute by placing another piece into current mosaic of quantum understanding of the world around us. We are aware that this is not an easy task. Honestly, though, what is more important for scientific development than positing new, challenging questions and seeking their possible answers? Perhaps nothing so much so.

We are closing this book with a wish. A wish that science shall be maximally vital and open to new thoughts. And, at the same time, we are also optimistically believing that contemporary science has already started to be just this!

Glossary

Absolute emptiness see the terms "emptiness" and "empty set".

Actuality is the empirical domain of our reality including systems and entities that have been actualized in time and space (and can be observed by a human observer).

Affective resonance is a dynamic entanglement between emotional states of two or more individuals. The emotions of an individual are suggested to influence the course of social interaction, as well as the emotions of the interaction partner or partners.

Agency beyond agency is the agency of an attractor or attractors responsible for quantum patterning in the initial stages of existence, as well as for the further development of systems, i.e. man, cultures, and societies.

Agency – collective – see the term "collective agency".

Agency – individual – is the potential (or capacity) of an autonomous individual to act, i.e. the ability of an individual to change reality, organize future situations, or change resource distribution. A temporarily constructed engagement by actors of different structural environments, which, through the interplay of habit, imagination, and judgment, both reproduces and transforms those structures in an interactive response to the problems posed by changing historical situations.

Altered state of consciousness is a state which is significantly different from a normative waking beta wave state. Such states can be experienced while dreaming during sleep, in lucid dreaming, trance states, hypnosis, meditation, during sensory deprivation, clinical death, or during intoxication by psychoactive drugs.

Alterity is otherness, the difference between the quality and state of being in the sense of the other of two.

Angular momentum is a vector quantity that can be used to describe the overall state of a physical system or a particle. Vector quantity is a quantity which has both magnitude and direction. For a rigid body rotating around an axis of symmetry, angular momentum can be expressed as the product of the body's moment of inertia (a measurement of an object's resistance to changes in its rotation rate) and its angular velocity.

Archetypes are primary, unobservable, and irreducible elements of collective unconscious (in Jung's sense). Archetypes are suggested to be completely invisible and appear only symbolically in dreams, fantasies, and altered states of consciousness in the form of primordial archetypal images.

Aristotelian potentiality Aristotle distinguished between potentiality (*dynamis*) and actuality (*energeia*). Potentiality is a group of things that continues without terminating, continuing or repeating itself over and over again with no recognizable ending point.

Attractor is the constellation, equilibrium state, or cycle of states towards which a system tends to move. At the moment of its emergence, the attractor provides the initial information for a new, arising system. In the field of quantum anthropology, attractors are understood as agentic constellations that are responsible for the initial variability among individuals, as well as among various forms of social coherence.

Autopoiesis is a self-producing mechanism which maintains the identity and existence of a system, through self-reference, self-regulation, and feedback.

Autopoietical reproduction refers to the self-reproduction, self-realization, and self-evolvement of a complex system. All systems are continually self-producing, and autopoiesis is present in most complex systems.

Brane is a fundamental concept in string theory. A brane (abbreviation for membrane) is an object which can have any number of allowed dimensions.

Cellular consciousness signifies the functions and operations of the cell membrane. The cell membrane is the boundary between the external physical environment and the internal environment of the cell. Its function is to interpret the stimuli and signals from the external environment via cellular receptors in the membrane surface. Receptors operate to identify and "connect" only with certain stimuli of either a physical, chemical, or energetic signature or configuration, and then translate that reality into an internal message, instruction, or reaction inside the cell.

(159)

Coherence see the terms "quantum coherence" and "social coherence".

Collapse of wave function see the terms "wave function collapse" and "uncollapsed wave function".

Collective agency is a supra-individual, collective potential (or capacity) that acts to change reality. Collective agency is the active element of each culture. Collective agency depends on social relations for its actualization in time and space.

Collective body refers to the synchronization in behavior and emotional arousal during collective ritual practices. In the course of a ritual, the internal biological rhythms of the participants become synchronized with the external rhythms produced by the ritual performance. This synchronization is enabled mostly by the synchronized repetitive physical actions of ritual participants.

Collective consciousness is a field that emerges based on some process of quantum binding between two or more individual consciousness (e.g. quantum entanglement). During such quantum binding, the fields of individual consciousness transcend the borders of the individual and interfere with the consciousness of another person or persons.

Collective effervescence is a kind of collective feeling that may emerge when members of a social group simultaneously communicate the same thought or participate in the same action. Collective effervescence excites individuals and serves to unify the group.

Collective memory is the shared memory that forms the ties that bind members of a group or society together. A social group's identity is constructed with narratives and traditions that are created to give its members a sense of community. Collective memory is shared, passed on, and also constructed by the group or society.

Collective unconscious is the background knowledge we have of which we are not aware when we are in normal states of consciousness. It is a transcendental dimension of our reality, common for all individuals and cultural groups. This system of a collective, universal nature involves pre-existent forms, a set of primary, unobservable, and irreducible elements called archetypes.

Complementarity principle no single perspective or view of a system can provide complete knowledge of the system. Therefore, understanding is always improving when additional perspectives are added. Each additional perspective or view of a system will reveal additional truths about the issue under investigation. Thus, the depth of understanding is a function of time and the number of perspectives.

Confusion of equivocation see the term "equivocation".

Contingency is the status of facts that are logically not necessarily true or necessarily false. Contingency is opposed to necessity – a contingent act is an act which could have not been, an act which is not necessary (could not have not been). Contingency differs from possibility, in a formal sense, as the latter includes statements which are necessarily true as well as not necessarily false, while a statement cannot be said to be contingent if it is necessarily true.

Cultural system is an informational spectrum shared by some of the members of a given social system. A cultural system consists of shared patterns and informational structures, i.e. shared ideas, rules, and symbols, and other cultural elements. Culture may manifest itself in various forms. Some forms of manifestation have a material appearance (material culture), whereas others are observable through human action in the world (the behavioral domain of cultural manifestations).

Cultural elements are, for example, shared thoughts, beliefs, assumptions, attitudes, preferences, values, standards and interpretations, shared behavioral rules, norms, social scripts, prototypical actions, normative patterns of behavior, customs, habits, practices, ceremonies, and rituals.

Cytoskeleton is a system of filaments or fibers that is present in the cytoplasm of eukaryotic cells (cells containing a nucleus). The cytoskeleton organizes other constituents of the cell, maintains the cell's shape, and is responsible for the locomotion of the cell itself and the movement of the various organelles within it.

D-branes are a special and important subset of branes defined by the condition that fundamental strings can end on the D-branes. D-branes also vibrate, but because their tension goes to infinity, even more energy is needed to excite these vibrations than for the strings. The quanta of these vibrations are particles identified with open strings – that move along these D-branes, but are stuck on them.

Decoherence see the term "quantum decoherence".

Deconstruction is a process of exploring the categories and concepts in various texts. Each word and, by extension, each text contains layers of meanings which have originated through cultural and historical processes. Through deconstructive reading, it is possible to reveal hidden meanings in texts. In such ways, texts may be deconstructed by the reader.

Deconstructive reading see the term "deconstruction".

Differentiation is the act or process of differentiating that perpetually proceeds inside all systems. We distinguish internal (inside the system) and external (system versus its environment) differentiation.

(161)

Discourse is a term used in linguistics to refer to a continuous stretch of language larger than a sentence. It includes both written and spoken communications. Critical discourse analysis consists of studying the relationship between discourse events, as well as sociopolitical or cultural factors.

Discursive acts are actions or events that occur in a particular discourse.

Discursive practices are the tools by which cultural meanings are produced and understood.

Domain of actuality see the term "actuality".

Domain of potentiality see the term "potentiality".

Embodiment – in theory of practice – is a metaphor mirroring the process of acquisition of cultural capital by individuals.

Embodiment – in quantum anthropology – man is seen to be an embodiment of a part of the overall wave-particle energy-information potential.

Emotional contagion is a process of transmitting internal emotional states between two or more individuals.

Empirical reality is the realm of actuality including already actualized systems and entities. Objects and entities of the empirical reality can be observed by our senses.

Emptiness refers to a hypothetical state that is absolutely empty. It is the possibility for the emergence of anything and everything – all objects, acts, practices, and events.

Empty set is a mesophase between absolute emptiness and actualization in time and space. The empty set is a phase when a sign enters into the range of concrete possibilities. It is something like the "noticed absence" of something that was or could have been or might possibly be there partially or wholly to fill the unoccupied space.

Entanglement, generally, is the kind of relationship that can be also called interlinking or interconnection. See also the term "quantum entanglement".

Equivocation refers to the possibility of participating in the alternative realities of two different cultures. Such equivocations should stimulate the attention of an anthropologist towards the relativistic interpretation of an investigated culture.

Experience of alterity see the term "horizontally extended experience".

Extension of consciousness see the term "vertical extension of consciousness".

Extra-corporeal experience see the term "out-of-body experience".

Fields see the terms "social fields" and "quantum field".

Fractal structure is a structure that consists of fractals. Generally, a fractal is a rough or fragmented geometric shape that can be split into parts, each of which is (at least approximately) a reduced-size copy of the whole.

Free will is a capacity of individuals to choose consciously and deliberately a course of action from among various alternatives.

Gene regulatory networks are a set of genes, or parts of genes, that interact with each other to control a specific cell function. Gene regulatory networks are important for development, for differentiation, and for responding to environmental cues.

Gradient of information is the rate (or slope) of change in information quantity in relation to changes in another variable.

Gravitation vector is a vector physical quantity which characterizes the gravitational field at a given point.

Group mind is the entanglement of emotions, cognitions, and incentives, constituting the collective consciousness of a group of individuals.

Hegel's absolute spirit is spirit not limited by anything else other than itself and its own stage of development. Absolute spirit is the goal, aim, or target of the force, as well as the reflection (realization) of the targets.

Heterogeneous inner dynamics is a source of differentiation, diversity, and multiplicity. It is a primary source of alterity in the world. Heterogeneous inner dynamics stimulates change and the creation of various things. It stimulates production and disrupts sameness.

Hilbert space is a theoretical vector function space with an infinite number of possible dimensions.

Homogeneous inner dynamics is generally characterized by an invariance and a tendency to return things to their original state of order, i.e. to the very beginning of their existence.

Horizontally extended experience (horizontal extension of consciousness) is the shift between realities of various cultures, i.e. between different cultural mentalities. The researcher shifts his/her perspective and tries to understand another culture through the internal logic of this culture.

Inner dynamics – general dynamics potentiating the processes in a system and affecting the life trajectory of a system in a specific direction.

Interference is the process in which two or more activities of systems or fields of the same quality combine to reinforce or cancel each other. See also the term "quantum interference".

(163)

Intra-acting agencies means the mutual interaction between the observer, the observed, and the apparatus used in the moment of observation.

Isomorphism is similarity in the form or in the general pattern of the structure or behavior of a system.

Local-global coupling is a kind of coupling between the local level of individual consciousness and global level of collective consciousness.

Magnetic moment is a measure of the strength and the direction of magnetism of a system or a particle.

Morphogenesis is formation of the structure of an organism or part.

Mytheme is the essential kernel of a myth. It represents an irreducible, unchanging element, a minimal unit that is always found in entanglement with other, related mythemes.

Mythopoeia is a myth-making process present in a cultural system. It includes scientific beliefs, traditional beliefs, fiction, artificial stories in literature, film, or other kinds of arts, and myths diffused by the internet and global media.

Mythopoeic system is a society's entire corpus of sacred cosmological symbolism, including the symbolism found in myth, ritual, mobiliary and architectural arts, drama, performance, sacred landscape, and games.

Neuterogeneous inner dynamics maintains harmony, order, and basically serves to protect the existence and the stability of a system. Neuterogeneous inner dynamics preserves quantum coherence in various existing systems. It also ensures an equilibrium between the homogeneous and the heterogeneous inner dynamics.

Nonempirical reality (or nonempirical domain) is the realm that contains the pre-existing empirical possibilities or virtual states that can be actualized in the empirical world.

Nonlinear quantum system is a system in which the output is not directly proportional to the input. Nonlinear systems are chaotic, unpredictable, and cannot be decomposed into parts and reassembled into the initial state. The oscillations of such systems are described by nonlinear equations.

Non-locality is the quantum principle that suggests that the universe is in fact profoundly different from our habitual understanding of it, and that the parts of the universe that we commonly consider to be separate, based on our everyday sensory experience, are actually potentially connected in an intimate and immediate way. The principle of non-locality stands against the paradigm of classic, Newtonian physics, where distant objects cannot have direct influence on one another, and that an object is directly influenced only by its immediate surroundings.

Observer effect means that the act of observing will influence the phenomenon being observed.

Ontological perspectivism see the terms "ontological turn" and "perspectival anthropology".

Ontological turn is the wave of relativistic studies in sociocultural anthropology with an accent on the sensitive investigation of differences between cultural ontologies, differences in the cultural understanding of the nature of being, becoming, existence, and reality.

Out-of-body experience is characterized by a feeling of departing from one's physical body and observing both one's self and the world from outside one's body, i.e. from an external perspective. This experience is quite common in dreams, daydreams, memories, during drug or anesthetic intoxication, and near-death experiences.

Overall, wave-particle energy-information potential is an underlying all-pervasive structure that provides energy-information potential for all actualizations in time and space. It is analogical to the idea of the "quantum sea" that is used in the field of quantum mechanics.

Peak experiences are transcendent experiences of heightened joy, awe, elation, ecstasy, or wonder. These are moments that stand out from all other ordinary everyday experiences. Peak experiences are characterized by an intensity of perception, depth of feeling, or sense of profound significance. During a peak experience, people feel at one with the world, and often experience a sense of losing track of time. Peak experiences lead to an increase in personal awareness and understanding, and can serve as a turning point in a person's life.

Perspectival anthropology (or perspectivism) is a relativistic anthropological concept originally coined by Viveiros de Castro, highlighting the different cultural points of view for anthropological analysis.

Platonic forms are the non-local and atemporal essences of various objects. They are unchanging underlying patterns, not located in space or time, that may cause plural representations of itself in particular objects. These forms are the essential basis of reality, which even means that they are superordinate to matter. Platonic forms are non-physical, non-empirical, non-visible, eternal, and changeless.

Platonic ideas are basically similar to Platonic forms, but, for example, Carter connects Platonic ideas with the abstract mind (formless imagery) and Platonic forms with the rational mind (rational and logical thinking).

Potentiality is a hidden, invisible domain of nonempirical, pre-existing possibilities.

Primordial images are appearances of archetypes to human consciousness, e.g. during dreams, fantasies, or altered states of consciousness. They are expressions of archetypes in time and space.

Probabilistic logic is the formal study of reasoning, working for example with different probabilities of occurrences of events in time and space.

Probability wave is a quantum state of a particle or system, characterized by a wave propagating through space in which the square of the magnitude of the wave at any given point corresponds to the probability of finding the particle at that point. Mathematically, a probability wave is described by the wave function, which is a solution to the wave equation describing the system. See also the terms "quantum state" and "quantum wave function".

Qualia are the subjective qualitative properties of experiences. They are the products of cognitive processing of sensory percepts. Qualia may be based on percepts coming from the external environment, but they are always subjective, because they emerge inside an individual.

Quantum anthropology is an anthropological perspective approaching man, culture, and humanity by taking into account the quantum nature of our reality. It is a meta-ontology explaining the basic categories of man's being in the world with the principles provided by quantum theory and quantum mechanics.

Quantum coherence is the physical condition of two or more particles or systems being in the same quantum state.

Quantum consciousness is the idea that consciousness requires quantum processes and that the underlying human consciousness is quantum in nature.

Quantum decoherence is the loss of coherence or ordering between the components of a system in a quantum superposition. By the loss of coherence, a system's behavior changes from that which can be explained by quantum mechanics to that which can be explained by classic mechanics.

Quantum entanglement is the kind of relationship where the quantum states of two or more objects have to be described with reference to each other, even though the individual objects may be spatially separated.

Quantum field is basically the sum of all wave function possibilities. Everything consists of energy and therefore produces a wave. All of these waves together interfere with each other and create new combinations of waves. Sometimes, particular waves increase in their amplitude and sometimes waves completely disappear. Everything contributes to infecting the quantum field. Every thought, every feeling, and every human action has its effect in the quantum field.

Quantum interference is a situation where two or more particles that are space and time independent interact, constructing or destructing their wave functions. This is a variation of wave amplitude that occurs from the superposition of two or more waves.

Quantum patterning is the process that is present when an entity comes into existence from the overall, wave-particle energy-information potential. Quantum patterning creates a network of quantum entanglements and superpositions for the future existence of a particular entity.

Quantum sea is the single underlying structure that is common for the entire universe and consists of so-called zero-point fluctuations in the vacuum. This all-pervasive energetic field, also called quantum vacuum energy, or zero-point energy, is a random, ambient fluctuating energy that exists even in so-called empty space. A vacuum is never particle-free or field-free, but consists of continuous virtual particle-pair creation and annihilation processes. There are fleeting electromagnetic waves and pairs of microparticles that perpetually come into being and return back into nonexistence. Energy patterns, such as material entities or other entities, emerge as a result of the patterning of otherwise random, ambient zero-point energy. Sustained zero-point energy is continually being absorbed and re-emitted on a dynamic-balance basis. The quantum sea is analogical to the idea of the "overall, wave-particle energy-information potential" that is used in the field of quantum anthropology.

Quantum state is the condition in which a physical system exists, usually described by a wave function. A quantum state encodes an experimenter's knowledge or information about some aspect of reality. A quantum state provides a probability distribution for the value of each observable, i.e. for the outcome of each possible measurement of the system. Quantum states allow the system to be in a few states simultaneously, in what is called a "quantum superposition".

Quantum superposition is the idea that particles exist in multiple quantum states simultaneously. A subatomic particle can exist anywhere where it is not detected, i.e. where not being observed. The quantum wave function describing a particle is the sum of all possible wave functions multiplied by their relative probabilities. When the particle

(167)

is observed, the wave function collapses and only one quantum state of the particle appears in the moment of measurement.

Quantum wave function is the mathematical description of the wave characteristics of a particle. The value of the wave function of a particle at a given point of space and time is related to the likelihood of the particle's being there at the time.

Realm of actuality see the term "actuality".

Realm of zero states see the term "overall, wave-particle energy-information potential".

Realm of nonexistence see the terms "overall, wave-particle energy-information potential", "emptiness", and "empty set".

Realm of potentiality see the term "potentiality".

Scalar field is a region with a number assigned to each point. In a scalar field, the value of any point (in space, or on a surface, or wherever the field is defined) is a scalar, that is, a single number representing the magnitude of the field at that point.

Self-organization is the ability of a system to spontaneously arrange its components or elements in a purposeful (non-random) manner, under the appropriate conditions, but without the help of an external agency.

Semiosis is an action or process involving the establishment of a relationship between a sign, its object and meaning.

Single point attractor is an attractor where all orbits in phase space are drawn to one point, or value. A system that is attracted by single point attractor heads towards the point where velocity and position are equal to zero.

Social aggregate is analogy of social system.

Social coherence is the quality or state of social cohering between people. Social coherence refers to social cohesiveness, cooperation, and the willingness to coordinate individual efforts between the members of a social system.

Social fields – in theory of practice – are structured social spaces existing in various cultural settings, e.g. religion, arts, or education.

Sociocultural meta-system is an all-encompassing complex that covers both social and cultural totality. It is the overall sociocultural reality, and various forms of observations may bring different insights based on the perspective and apparatus used.

Social system is a nonlinear, highly complex quantum system composed of temporary interrelationships between its elements, i.e. individuals and groups. Social bonds in social systems are perpetually changing in the sense of the ongoing reconfiguration of their structure.

Social unit is analogy of social system.

Strange attractor is the limit set of a chaotic trajectory. A strange attractor is an attractor that is topologically distinct from a periodic orbit or a limit cycle.

String theory is a theory which says that everything in the universe is made up of very tiny vibrating strings. These strings vibrate in the four dimensions of spacetime and in additional, hypothetical, spacelike dimensions. On distance scales larger than the string scale, a string looks like an ordinary particle, with its mass, charge, and other properties determined by vibrational state of the string.

Superposition see the term "quantum superposition".

Synchronization between minds occurs, for example, during collective rituals and trance states. During this entanglement between minds, people experience similar emotions, feelings, and perceptions.

Temporalization of complexity is the process of the constitution of system's complexity in time. The temporalization of complexity proceeds through the temporalization of system's elements. A system's elements perpetually emerge and then die after some time. The occurrence of one element makes the future emergence of others either more probable or more improbable.

Temporalized complexity is time-dependent complexity including the flexibility of a system's structures enabling a change in a complex and fluctuating environment.

Transcendence is the act of rising above something to a superior state by going beyond the limits of ordinary experience. The word is often used to describe a spiritual or religious state, or a condition of moving beyond physical needs and realities. See also the term "peak experiences".

Uncollapsed wave function if the collapse of a wave function does not occur, the wave spreads out over the entire space.

Vector is a quantity or phenomenon that has two independent properties: magnitude and direction.

Vector field is a region where the value of any point (in space, or on a surface, or wherever the field is defined) is a vector, meaning that the value has both a magnitude and a direction.

Vertical extension of consciousness (or vertically extended experience) means the extension of human consciousness to some extra dimensions experienced during altered states of consciousness. These extra dimensions have special qualities other than the qualities of our common reality experienced during normal states of consciousness.

(169)

See also the terms "altered state of consciousness" and "peak experiences".

Wave function see the term "quantum wave function".

Wave function collapse according to the classic Copenhagen Interpretation, it is a jump in the state of a particle that occurs in the moment of measurement. In the wave function collapse, one of the possible quantum states is actualized in time and space.

More recently, wave function collapse is understood as an approximation to the phenomenon of "quantum decoherence".

Wave-particle complementarity means that every particle or entity exhibits the properties of not only particles, but also of waves. According to wave-particle complementarity, all objects have complementary properties, which cannot be measured accurately at the same time.

Wave-particle duality see the term "wave-particle complementarity".

Zero-point fluctuations see the term "quantum sea".

Zero state see the terms "emptiness" and "empty set".

References

Aerts, D. (2010). Interpreting quantum particles as conceptual entities. *International Journal of Theoretical Physics, 49*(12), 2950–2970.

Alberti, B., Fowles, S., Holbraad, M., Marshall, Y., & Witmore, C. (2011). Worlds otherwise: Archaeology, anthropology, and ontological difference. *Current Anthropology, 52*(6), 896–912.

Alcorta, C. S., & Sosis, R. (2005). Ritual, emotion and sacred symbols: The evolution of religion as an adaptive complex. *Human Nature – An Interdisciplinary Biosocial Perspective, 16*(4), 323–359.

d'Aquili, E. G., Laughlin, C. D., & McManus, J. (1979). *The spectrum of ritual.* New York: Columbia University Press.

Arrow, H., & Burns, K. L. (2004). Self-organizing culture: How norms emerge in small groups. In M. Schaller & C. S. Crandall (Eds.), *The psychological foundation of culture* (171–199). London: Lawrence Erlbaum Associates.

Atmanspacher, H. (2004). Quantum theory and consciousness: An overview with selected examples. *Discrete Dynamics in Nature and Society*, 1, 51–73.

Bacigalupo, A. M. (1998). The exorcising sounds of warfare: The Performance of shamanic healing and the struggle to remain Mapuche. *Anthropology of Consciousness, 9*(2–3), 1–16.

Bacigalupo, A. M. (2014). The potency of indigenous "bibles" and biographies: Mapuche shamanic literacy and historical consciousness. *American Ethnologist, 41*(4), 648–663.

Balcar, K., Kuška, M., & Trnka, R. (2011). Bolest jako lék? [Pain as a cure?]. *Bolest, 14*(3), 139–146.

Barad, K. (2007). *Meeting the Universe halfway: Quantum physics and entanglement of matter and meaning.* London: Duke University Press.

Bárta, M. (2013). Kolaps a regenerace: Pokračující cesty minulých civilizací. [Collapse and regeneration: Continuing the path of past civilizations]. In M. Bárta & M. Kovář (Eds.), *Kolaps a regenerace: Cesty ci-*

vilizací a kultur: Minulost, současnost a budoucnost komplexních společností (19–46). Prague: Academia.

Barth, F. (1969). Introduction. In F. Barth (Ed.), *Ethnic groups and boundaries* (9–38). Prospect Heights: Waveland Press.

Barthes, R. (1993). *Mythologies*. London: Vintage Classics.

Bateson, G. (1972). *Steps to an ecology of mind*. New York: Bellantine.

Baudrillard, J. (1995). *Simulacra and simulation*. Ann Arbor: University of Michigan Press.

Belaunde, L. E. (2008). The reason for the body: Ideology of the body and representation of the environment in the Mirana of Amazonian Colombia. *Journal of the Royal Anthropological Institute, 14*(2), 448–450.

Benenti, G., Casati, G., & Strini, G. (2004). *Principles of quantum computation and information*. Volume I: Basic concepts. Singapore: World Scientific Publishing.

Bergallo, G. E. (2002). The interpretative foundations of culture: Quantum aesthetics and anthropology. In M. J. Caro & J. W. Murphy (Eds.), *The world of quantum culture* (145–164). Westport: Praeger.

Berger, J. (2011). Arousal increases social transmission of information. *Psychological Science, 22*(7), 891–893.

Berger, P. L., & Luckmann, T. (1966). *The social construction of reality: A treatise in the sociology of knowledge*. London: Penguin Books.

Bhattacharya, R., Tiwari, A., Fung, J., & Murray, R. M. (2009). Cone invariance and rendezvous of multiple agents. Proceedings of the Institution of Mechanical Engineers, Part G. *Journal of Aerospace Engineering, 223*, 779–789.

Bhullar, N. (2012). Relationship between mood and susceptibility to emotional contagion: Is positive mood more contagious? *North American Journal of Psychology, 14*(3), 517–529.

Bohm, D. (1980). *Wholeness and implicate order*. London: Routledge and Kegan Paul.

Bohr, N. (1928). The quantum postulate and the recent development of atomic theory. *Nature, 121*(3050), 580–590.

Bourdieu, P. (1977). *Outline of a theory of practice*. Cambridge: Cambridge University Press.

Brentano, F. (1995). *Psychology from an empirical standpoint*. London: Routledge.

Bundgaard, P. F. (2013). Roman Ingarden's theory of reader experience: A critical assessment. *Semiotica, 194*, 171–188.

Carter, P. J. (2014). Consciousness in higher-dimensional quantum space-time. *NeuroQuantology, 12*(1), 46–75.

Casti, J. L. (1994). *Complexification: Explaining a paradoxical world through the science of surprise*. New York: Harper Collins.

Chrzanowska-Kluczewska, E. (2015). Textual indeterminacy revisited: From Roman Ingarden onwards. *Journal of Literary Semantics, 44*(1), 1–21.

Collins, R. (2004). *Interaction ritual chains*. Princeton: Princeton

Combs, A., & Krippner, S. (2008). Collective consciousness and the social brain. *Journal of Consciousness Studies, 15*(10–11), 264–276.

Derrida, J. (1997). *Of grammatology*. Baltimore: Johns Hopkins University Press.

Davisson, C., & Germer, L. H. (1927). Differaction of electrons by a crystal of nickel. *Physical Review, 30*(6), 705–741.

Drackle, D. (1999). Living and dying: Images of death and mourning in the Alentejo (Portugal). *Anthropos, 94*(1–3), 121–140.

Durkheim, E. (1997). *The division of labor in society*. New York: Free Press.

Eccles, J. C. (1994). *How the self controls its brain*. New York: Springer-Verlag.

Einstein, A. (1920). *Relativity: The special and general theory*. New York: H. Holt & Comp.

Enfield, N. J. (2005). The body as a cognitive artifact in kinship representations: Hand gesture diagrams by speakers of Lao. *Current Anthropology, 46*(1), 51–81.

Feinberg, R., & Genz, J. (2012). Limitations of language for conveying navigational knowledge: Way-finding in the Southeastern Solomon Islands. *American Anthropologist, 114*(2), 336–350.

Fischbeck, H.-J. (2005). *Die Wahrheit und das Leben – Wissenschaft und Glaube im 21. Jahrhundert* [Truth and life – Science and faith in the 21st century]. München: Utz Verlag.

Foerster, von H. (1988). On constructing a reality. In S. C. Feinstein, A. H. Esman, J. G. Looney & G. H. Orvin, *Adolescent psychiatry*. Vol. 15, Developmental and clinical studies (77–95). Chicago: University of Chicago Press.

Foucault, M. (1970). *The order of things: An archaeology of the human sciences*. New York: Pantheon Books.

Foucault, M. (1972). *Archaeology of knowledge*. New York: Pantheon Books.

Geertz, C. (1973). *Interpretation of culture*. New York: Basic Books.

Gelman, S. A., & Legare, C. H. (2011). *Concepts and folk theories. Annual Review of Anthropology, 40,* 379–398.

Grandpierre, A. (1997). The physics of collective consciousness. World futures. *The Journal of General Evolution, 48*(1–4), 23–56.

Hameroff, S. (1998) Quantum computation in brain microtubules? The Penrose-Hameroff "Orch OR" Model of Consciousness. *Philosophical Transactions of the Royal Society London, 356,* 1869–1896.

Hameroff, S., & Penrose, R. (1996). Orchestrated reduction of quantum coherence in brain microtubules: A model for consciousness? In S. R. Hameroff, A. W. Kaszniak & A. C. Scott (Eds.), *Toward a science of consciousness – The first Tucson discussions and debates* (507–540). Cambridge: MIT Press.

Hameroff, S., & Penrose, R. (2014). Consciousness in the Universe: A review of the 'Orch OR' theory. *Physics of Life Reviews, 11*(1), 39–78.

Hampton, O. W. (1999). *Culture of stone: Sacred and profane uses of stone among the Dani.* College Station: Texas A&M University Press.

Harris, O. J. T., & Robb, J. (2012). Multiple ontologies and the problem of the body in history. *American Anthropologist, 114*(4), 668–679.

Harrison, S. (2004). Emotional climates: Ritual, seasonality and affective disorders. *Journal of the Royal Anthropological Institute, 10*(3), 583–602.

Hatfield, E., Cacioppo, J. T., & Rapson, R. L. (1994). *Emotional contagion.* Paris: Cambridge University Press.

Heidegger, M. (1962). *On time and being.* New York: Harper and Row.

Heidegger, M. (1996). *Being and time.* Albany: SUNY Press.

Heisenberg, W. (1958). *Physik und Philosophie.* Stuttgart: Hirzel.

Hester, P. T., & Adams, K. M. G. (2014). *Systemic thinking: Fundamentals for understanding problems and messes.* New York: Springer.

Hodgson, D. (1991). *The mind matters: Consciousness and choice in a quantum world.* Oxford: Clarendon Press.

Holland, D., Lachicotte, W., Skinner, D., & Cain, C. (2003). *Identity and agency in cultural worlds.* Cambridge: Harvard University Press.

Holmberg, D. (2006). Transcendence, power and regeneration in Thmang shamanic practice. *Critique of Anthropology, 26*(1), 87–101.

Husserl, E. (1964). *The idea of phenomenology.* The Hague: Nijhoff.

Husserl, E. (1983). *Ideas pertaining to a pure phenomenology and to a phenomenological philosophy.* First Book. Dordrecht: Kluwer.

Ingarden, R. (1973a). *The literary work of art.* Evanston: Northwestern University Press.

Ingarden, R. (1973b). *The cognition of the literary work of art.* Evanston: Northwestern University Press.

Ingarden, R. (1975). Phenomenological aesthetics: An attempt at defining its range. *The Journal of Aesthetics and Art Criticism, 33*(3), 257–269.

Ingold, T. (2005a). Introduction to culture. In T. Ingold (Ed.), *Companion encyclopedia of anthropology* (329–349). London: Routledge.

Ingold, T. (2005b). Introduction to social life. In T. Ingold (Ed.), *Companion encyclopedia of anthropology* (737–755). London: Routledge.

Isaeva, V. V. (2012). Self-organization in biological systems. *Biology Bulletin, 39*(2), 110–118.

Iurato, G. (2015). A brief comparison of the unconscious as seen by Jung and Levi-Strauss. *Anthropology of Consciousness, 26*(1), 60–107.

Johnson, C. (2003). *D-branes.* Cambridge: Cambridge University Press.

Judge, A. (1993). *Human values as strange attractors: Coevolution of classes of governance principles.* Paper presented in the 13th World Conference "Coherence and chaos in our uncommon futures – visions, means, actions" (Finland, August 1993) of the World Futures Studies Federation (WFSF).

Jung, C. G. (1959). *The archetypes and the collective unconscious.* Collected Works, Vol. 9, Part 1. Princeton: Princeton University Press.

Jung, C. G. (1983) *Man and his symbols.* New York: Windfall.

Kant, I. (2006). *Anthropology from a pragmatic point of view.* New York: Cambridge University Press.

Kiel, L. D., & Elliot, E. (Eds.) (2004). *Chaos theory in the social sciences: Foundations and applications.* Michigan: The University of Michigan Press.

Kirby, V. (2011). *Quantum anthropologies: Life at large.* London: Duke University Press.

Knox, J. (2003). *Archetype, attachment, analysis: Jungian psychology and the emergent mind.* New York: Brunner – Routledge.

Kockelman, P. (2007). Agency: The relation between meaning, power, and knowledge. *Current Anthropology, 48*(3), 375–401.

Kondratiev, N. D. (1935). The long waves in economic life. *The Review of Economic Statistics, 17*(6), 105–115.

Konvalinka, I., Xygalatas, D., Bulbulia, J., Schjoedt, U., Jegindo, E., Wallot, S., et al. (2011). Synchronized arousal between performers and related spectators in a fire-walking ritual. *Proceedings of the National Academy of Science (PNAS), 108*(2), 8514–8519.

Kuška, M., Trnka, R., & Balcar, K. (2013). Two decades of transformation of inequalities: New identities and new fears in the post-communist Czech society. In S. Wray, R. Rae (Eds.), *Personal and public lives and relationships in a changing social world* (104–114). Newcastle: Cambridge Scholars Publishing.

Kübler-Ross, E. (1992). *On death and dying: Questions and answers on death and dying.* New York: Quality Paperback Book Club.

Laszlo, E. (1995). *The interconnected Universe: Conceptual foundations of transdisciplinary unified theory.* Singapore: World Scientific.

Laughlin, C. D., & Throop, C. J. (2001). Imagination and reality: On the relations between myth, consciousness, and the quantum sea. *Zygon, 36*(4), 709–736.

Laughlin, C. D., McManus, J., & d'Aquili, E. G. (1990). *Brain. Symbol and experience: Toward a neurophenomenology of consciousness.* New York: Columbia University Press.

Lévi-Strauss, C. (1963). *Structural anthropology.* New York: Basic Books.

Lorencova, R. (2008) Pohřební rituály Benuaqů [The Benuaq funeral rituals]. Ph.D. dissertation, Charles University in Prague.

Lorencova, R. (2010/2011). *Spiritualita uživatelů alkoholu a marihuany* [Spirituality of alcohol and marijuana users]. Prague: Dauphin.

Luhmann, N. (1995). *Social systems.* Stanford: Stanford University Press.

Luhrmann, T. M. (2011). Hallucinations and sensory overrides. *Annual Review of Anthropology, 40,* 71–85.

Lyotard, J.-F. (1984). *The postmodern condition: A report on knowledge.* Manchester: Manchester University Press.

Malafouris, L. (2015). Metaplasticity and the primacy of material engagement. *Time & Mind – The Journal of Archaeology Consciousness and Culture, 8*(4), 351–371.

Malin, S. (2012). *Nature loves to hide: Quantum physics and the nature of reality, Western perspective.* London: World Scientific Publishing.

Marchand, T. H. J. (2010). Making knowledge: Explorations of the indissoluble relation between minds, bodies, and environment. *Journal of the Royal Anthropological Institue, 16,* Special Issue, S1–S21.

McCraty, R. (2002). *The energetic heart: Bioelectromagnetic Interactions within and between people.* Boulder Creek: HeartMath Research Center.

Mella, P. (2014). *The magic ring: Systems thinking approach to control systems.* New York: Springer.

Mensky, M. B. (2010). *Consciousness and quantum mechanics: Life in parallel worlds – miracles of consciousness from quantum reality.* Singapore: World Scientific Publishing.

Merrell, F. (2009). Sign, mind, time, space: Contradictory complementary coalescence. *Semiotica, 177*(1–4), 29–116.

Midgley, D. (2006). Intersubjectivity and collective consciousness. *Journal of Consciousness Studies, 13*(5), 99–109.

Miller, D. (Ed.) (1998). *Material cultures: Why some things matter*. London: University of Chicago Press.

Moody, R. (1975). *Life after life: And reflections on life after life*. Guideposts: Carmel.

Moore, L. (2015). Fileds of the networked mind: Ritual consciousness and the factor of communitas in networked rites of compassion. *Technoetic Arts: A Journal of Speculative Research, 43*(3), 331–339.

Moran, D. (2000). *Introduction to phenomenology*. London: Routledge.

Murphy, G. (1945). Field theory and survival. *Journal of the American Society for Psychical Research, 39*(2), 181–209.

Mühlhoff, R. (2015). Affective resonance and social interaction. *Phenomenology and the Cognitive Sciences, 14*(4), 1001–1019

Neiger, A. (2003). The narrated body: The representation of corporeality in contemporary literature. In L. Fortunati, J. E. Katz & R. Riccini (Eds.), *Mediating the human body: Technology, communication, and fashion* (51–59). Mahwah: Lawrence Erlbaum Associates Publishers.

Neumann, R., Strack, F. (2000). "Mood contagion": The automatic transfer of moods between persons. *Journal of Personality and Social Psychology, 79*(2), 211–223.

Özkan, T. S. (2012). Theoretical Approaches on the faith element of healing under traditional medicine, psychosomatic medicine, placebo effect, quantum healing. *Milli Folklor, 24*(95), 307–314.

Paleček, M., & Risjord, M. (2012). Relativism and the ontological turn within anthropology. *Philosophy of the Social Sciences, 43*(1), 3–23.

Pattee, H. H. (2013). Epistemic, evolutionary, and physical conditions for biological information. *Biosemiotics, 6*(1), 9–31.

Paulson, S., Kellehear, A., Kripal J. J., & Leary L. (2014). Confronting mortality: Faith and meaning across cultures. *Annals of the New York Academy of Sciences, 1330*, 58–74.

Penniman, N. (2002). Rhythm and movement in Ghana: Healing through dance through generations. *African Diaspora ISPs*, Paper 47.

Pownell, S. (1996). Quantum anthropology. *Anthropology News, 37*(4), 2.

Pusey, M. F., Barrett, J., & Rudolph, T. (2012). On the reality of the quantum state. *Nature Physics, 8*, 475–478.

Puthoff, H. E. (2002). Searching for the universal matrix in metaphysics. *Research News and Opportunities in Science and Theology, 2*(8), 22–24.

Rigas, I., Sánchez-Soto, L. L., Klimov, A.,B., Řeháček, J., & Hradil, Z. (2008). Full quantum reconstruction of vortex states. *Physical Review, A78*(6), 060101(R).

Rappaport, R. (1999). *Ritual and religion in the making of humanity*. Cambridge: Cambridge University Press.

Roberts, N. (2012). Is conversion a 'colonization of consciousness'? *Anthropological Theory, 12*(3), 271–294.

Roberts, R. H. (2006). Body. In R. A. Segal (Ed.), *The Blackwell Companion to the study of religion* (213–228). Oxford: Blackwell Publishing.

Rolin, K. (2009). Standpoint theory as a methodology for the study of power relations. *Hypatia, 24*(4), 218–226.

Roll, W. G. (1965). The psi field. In W. Roll & J. G. Pratt (Eds.), *Proceedings of the Parapsychological Association* (32–65). Durham: Parapsychological Association.

Rosenblum, B., & Kuttner, F. (2006). *Quantum enigma: Physics encounters consciousness*. New York: Oxford University Press.

Russel, B. (2009). *Unpopular essays*. New York: Routledge.

Russell, H. A. (2013). Quantum anthropology: Reimaging the human person as body/spirit. *Theological Studies, 74*, 934–959.

Sahu, S., Ghosh, S., Hirata, K., Fujita, D., & Bandyopadhyay, A. (2013). Multi-level memory-switching properties of a single brain microtubule. *Applied Physics Letters, 102*, 123701.

Sarkar, R. M. (2002). Culture, ecology, and tradition: The interactional patterns in shaping the modes of behaviour in a primitive tribe. *Man in India, 82*(1–2), 5–22.

Sarsambekova, A. S., Karibaevna, B. S., & Saparkalievich, S. E. (2015). "Ata Zhol" in Kazakhstan: Spiritual revival through neo-shamanism. *Anthropologist, 20*(3), 462–467.

Sartre, J.-P. (1995). *Being and nothingness: An essay on phenomenological ontology*. London: Routledge.

Saunders, S., Barrett, J., Kent, A., & Wallace, D. (2010). *Many worlds? Everett, quantum theory, and reality*. New York: Oxford University Press.

Schäfer, L. (2006). Quantum reality and the consciousness of the Universe: Quantum reality, the emergence of complex order from virtual states and the importance of consciousness in the Universe. *Zygon, 41*(3), 505–532.

Schäfer, L. (2008). Nonempirical Reality: Transcending the physical and spiritual in the order of the one. *Zygon, 43*(2), 329–352.

Schiller, A. (1997). *Small sacrifices. Religious change and cultural identity among the Ngaju of Indonesia*. Oxford: Oxford Universiy Press.

Segal, R. A. (Ed.) (2006). *The Blackwell Companion to the study of religion*. Oxford: Blackwell Publishing.

Singer, T., & Lamm, C. (2009). The social neuroscience of empathy. *Annals of the New York Academy of Sciences, 1156*, 81–96.

Steffen, V. (2013). Crisis as deferred closure: Clairvoyant counselling in contemporary Danish society. *Anthropology & Medicine, 20*(2), SI, 190–202.

Stoeckigt, B. M. H., Besch, F., Jeserich, F., Holmberg, C., Witt, C. M., & Teut, M. (2015). Biographical similarities between spiritual sealers and their clients in Germany: A qualitative study. *Anthropology & Medicine, 22*(2), 177–190.

Thompson, P. J. (2000). *Creationism and evolution: A systems perspective on a textbook controversy.* Paper presented at the Annual Meeting of the American Educational Research Association, New Orleans, LA, April 24–28, 2000. Available at http://files.eric.ed.gov/fulltext/ED440874.pdf

Trnka, R. (2011). Sociable rule-adaptiveness in the evolution of human sociality: Peripheral and prototypical group memberships. *Anthropologie – International Journal of Human Diversity and Evolution, 2*, 165–169.

Trnka, R. (2013). How many dimensions does emotional experience have? The theory of multi-dimensional emotional experience. In R. Trnka, K. Balcar & M. Kuška (Eds.), *Re-constructing emotional spaces: From experience to regulation* (45–55). Saarbrücken: Lambert Academic Publishing.

Trnka, R. (2015a). In the chaos of today's society: The dynamics of collapse as another shift in the quantum anthropology of Heidi Ann Russell. In I. Rynda (Ed.), *Krize: Společnost, kultura a ekologie [Crisis: Society, culture, and ecology]* (11–34). Prague: Togga.

Trnka, R. (2015b). *Sociobiodiversity and the dynamics of human society.* Series of lectures held at the Faculty of the Humanities of Charles University in Prague.

Trnka, R., Lačev, A., Balcar, K., Kuška, M., & Tavel, P. (2016). Modeling semantic emotion space using a 3D hypercube-projection: An innovative analytical approach for the psychology of emotions. *Frontiers in Psychology, 7*(art. n. 522), 1–12.

Turchin, P. (2003). *Historical dynamics.* Princeton: Princeton University Press.

Turner, J. H., & Stets, J. E. (2005). *The sociology of emotions.* New York: Cambridge University Press.

Turner, V. (1969). *Liminality and communitas. The ritual process, structure and antistructure.* Chicago: Aldine Publishing.

Turner, V. (1982). *From ritual to theatre.* London: PAJ Publications.

Turner, V. (1990). Are there universals of performance in myth, ritual and drama? In R. Schechner & W. Appel (Eds.), *By means of performance* (8–18). Cambridge: Cambridge University Press.

Umpleby, S. A. (2007). Physical relationship among matter, energy and information. *Systems Research and Behavioral Science, 24*(3), 369–372.

Vann, E. F. (1995). Quantum ethnography: Anthropology in the post-Einsteinian era. *Lambda Alpha Journal, 25/26*, 71–80.

Venkatesen, S. (Ed.) (2010). Ontology is just another word for culture. Motion tabled at the 2008 Meeting of the Group for Debates in Anthropological Theory, University of Manchester. *Critique of Anthropology, 30*(2), 152–200.

Venz, O. (2013). *Die autochthone Religion der Benuaq von Ost-Kalimantan – eine ethnolinguistische Untersuchung*. Ph.D. dissertation. Albert-Ludwigs Universitat Freiburg.

Venz, O. (2014). Skulls, ancestors and the meaning of kelelungan: An ethnoliguistic look into the history of a key religious term of the Greater Luangan. *Borneo Research Bulletin, 45*, 257–298.

Viveiros de Castro, E. (2004). Perspectival anthropology and the method of controlled equivocation. *Tipití, 2*(1), 3–22.

Wagner, R. (1981). *The invention of culture*. Chicago: University of Chicago Press.

Weiner, N. (1961). *Cybernetics*. New York: MIT Press.

Wegner, D. M. (1987). Transactive memory: A contemporary analysis of the group mind. In B. Mullen & G. R. Goethals (Eds.), *Theories of group behavior* (185–208). New York: Springer.

Wendt, A. (2006). Social theory as cartesian science: An auto-critique from a quantum perspective. In S. Guzzini & A. Leander (Eds.), *Constructivism and international relations*. London: Routledge.

Wendt, A. (2015). *Quantum mind and social science: Unifying physical and social ontology*. Cambridge: Cambridge University Press.

Whitchurch, G. G., & Constantine, L. L. (1993). Systems theory. In P. Boss, W. J. Doherty, R. LaRossa, W. R. Schumm & S. K. Steinmetz (Eds.), *Sourcebook of family theories and methods: A contextual approach* (325–352). New York: Springer.

Yolles, M., Frieden, B. R., & Kemp, G. (2008). Toward a formal theory of socioculture: A yin-yang information-based theory of social change. *Kybernetes, 37*(7), 850–909.

Ziman, J. (2006). No man is an island. *Journal of Consciousness Studies, 13*(5), 17–42.

Index

(187)

ritual
- and consciousness 27, 37, 81–82, 136, 138
- and reality 38, 69, 79, 104, 132–136, 140–141, 144–145, 152
- and observer effect 136–138, 141–142
- entanglement 85, 132, 139–141, 150
- fire-walking 140–142
- funeral 69
- symbolism 138
rules – social 23, 63, 65, 98, 149

sacred 37–39, 124–127, 130, 132, 134, 139–141, 144
self-actualization 18, 78
self-consciousness 45
self-experience 105–106
self-mutilation 39–40
self-organization 55, 62, 126, 154, **168**
semantics 17–18, 59, 116–122, 125, 127–128, 130–134
semiosis 89, **168**
semiotics 18, 98, 117, 118, 120–122, 132
separatist movement 99–100
shaman 37, 39, 69, 82, 108, 133, 139, 144
Schäffer, L. 30, 57, 86, 118, 137, 143
signs 18, 98, 117, 118, 120–122, 132
simplification 97–100
Slavic 132–134
social
- aggregate 26, 52, 55, 58–59, 61, 91–103, 109, 112, 114, 146, 148, 151, **168**
- bonds 60, 148–149
- change 95–100, 103
- groups 25, 47, 56, 61, 95, 115, 148
- - and alterity 101, 154–157
- - coherence 80, 108–110, 150–151
- - membership 55–56, 61–64, 67, 71, 85–86, 100, 129, 149

- inequality 101
- interaction 61, 65, 67
- life 13, 59, 80
- organization 60–61
- reality – construction 16–17, 41
- science 12, 15, 20, 24–25, 157
- spaces 17
- structure 17, 60–61
- system – emergence 55–56
- - life trajectory 93, 101, 109, 120
- - in quantum anthropology 60–62, **168**
sociality 24
socialization 60, 75, 85, 121, 131
sociocultural
- anthropology – quantum turn 20
- complexity 58, 60
- dynamics 55, 67, 91–112, 149–150
- meta-system 59–60, 72, 148, **168**
- reality 26, 44–46, 48, 58–60, 92, 148
Soviet Union 98–100
space
- empty 49–50
- hyperspace 33
- objective 33
- three-dimensional 33–35, 111
speech act 69, 118–119
spirit – Hegel 30, **163**
standpoint (theory) 17, 29, 108
stereotypes 101
strange attractor 53–57, 90, 102, 114–115, **169**
string theory 33–37, 153, **169**
structural anthropology 22
structuralism 22, 87, 127
structuralism – isomorphism 21–22
structure
- dual 30
- informational 63
- language 64, 117, 121
- of myth 126
- symbolic 64
- universal 22, 126–128
- generic 22

(189)

Radek Trnka
Radmila Lorencová

Quantum Anthropology

Man, Cultures, and Groups
in a Quantum Perspective

Published by Charles University, Karolinum Press
Ovocný trh 5/560, 116 36 Prague 1, Czech Republic
www.karolinum.cz
Prague 2016
Edited by Jana Jindrová
Layout by Zdeněk Ziegler
Typeset by DTP Karolinum
Printed by Karolinum Press
First edition

ISBN 978-80-246-3470-8
ISBN 978-80-246-3526-2 (pdf)